THE NEW MERMAIDS

Doctor Faustus

THE NEW MERMAIDS

General Editors
BRIAN MORRIS
Professor of English Literature, University of Sheffield

BRIAN GIBBONS
Lecturer in English, University of York

ROMA GILL
Senior Lecturer in English Literature, University of Sheffield

Doctor Faustus

CHRISTOPHER MARLOWE

Edited by ROMA GILL

Senior Lecturer in English Literature,
University of Sheffield

17 30/22 65

ERNEST BENN LIMITED
LONDON & TONBRIDGE

First published in this form 1965
by Ernest Benn Limited
25 *New Street Square · London · EC*4*A* 3*JA &*
*Sovereign Way · Tonbridge · Kent · TN*9 1*RW*
Second (*corrected*) *impression* 1967
Third impression 1969
Fourth impression 1971
Fifth impression 1973
Sixth impression 1975
© *Ernest Benn Limited* 1965
Distributed in Canada by
The General Publishing Company Limited · Toronto
Printed in Great Britain
ISBN 0 510–33821–6 (*Paperback*)

IN MEMORY OF
MY MOTHER

CONTENTS

ACKNOWLEDGEMENTS

The greatest debt is to Sir Walter Greg for the massive achievement of his *Parallel Texts*. I am grateful to other modern editors for the examples they have set; to friends and colleagues who listened to me with constructive sympathy and patience; and to Professor Brockbank for his understanding and encouragement, as well as for his own work on the play. An allowance from the Sheffield University Research Fund enabled me to work from the original quartos in the British Museum and Bodleian Libraries.

Sheffield 1965   ROMA GILL

ABBREVIATIONS

I have followed the usual practice in referring to the seventeenth-century editions of *Dr. Faustus*. 'A' indicates substantial agreement among all the A texts which are referred to separately on occasion as A1 (1604), A2 (1609), and A3 (1611); the six B texts (1616, 1619, 1620, 1624, 1628, and 1631) are similarly distinguished. Modern editions consulted are referred to as follows:

Boas	*The Tragical History of Doctor Faustus*, edited by F. S. Boas (1923)
Bullen	*The Works of Christopher Marlowe*, edited by A. H. Bullen (1885)
Greg	*Marlowe's 'Dr. Faustus' 1604–1616: Parallel Texts*, edited by W. W. Greg (1950)
Jump	*Doctor Faustus*, edited by John D. Jump (1962)

Other works frequently referred to are:

EFB	The English *Faust Book*, the name often given to Marlowe's source [*The Historie of the damnable life, and deserved death of Doctor Iohn Faustus*, translated by P. F. (1592)]
Kocher	P. H. Kocher, *Christopher Marlowe* (Chapel Hill, 1946)
Tilley	M. P. Tilley, *A Dictionary of the Proverbs in England in the Sixteenth and Seventeenth Centuries* (Ann Arbor, 1950)

Names of periodicals are abbreviated:

E.L.H.	*English Literary History*
E.S.	*English Studies*
E & S	*Essays and Studies*
M.L.N.	*Modern Language Notes*
M.L.Q.	*Modern Language Quarterly*
M.L.R.	*Modern Language Review*
N & Q	*Notes and Queries*
P.Q.	*Philological Quarterly*
R.E.S.	*Review of English Studies*
T.L.S.	*Times Literary Supplement*

Quotations from other plays by Marlowe are taken from the edition of R. H. Case *et al.* (1930–33); those from Shakespeare's plays are from the London edition [edited by John Munro (1958)].

INTRODUCTION

THE AUTHOR

AT THE age of twenty-nine Marlowe was murdered. His death was welcomed by Her Majesty's Privy Council, which later pardoned the murderer, and by those popular moralists who hailed it as 'a manifest sign of God's judgement'[1] on a life of impiety and debauchery.

Marlowe was born into a turbulent Canterbury family. His father was a shoemaker of moderate means and excessive pugnacity, while two of his sisters, Dorothy and Ann, were notorious in the town—the former for various trade and matrimonial intrigues, the latter a noted 'scold, common swearer and blasphemer of the name of God'.[2] Marlowe escaped from the family's environment—though not, it would seem, from its characteristics—with the aid of those pious Elizabethans who had endowed scholarships for the encouragement of good learning in poor boys. The first scholarship, of £4 a year, took him to the King's School, Canterbury, from where he proceeded to Cambridge as a Matthew Parker scholar at Corpus Christi College. The Parker scholarship was awarded for three years in the first instance, and might be extended for a further three on evidence that the holder intended to take Holy Orders. Marlowe held his for the full six years. The College's Buttery Book shows him as an undergraduate whose expenditure easily exceeded his income but who from time to time spent nothing at all. There were, evidently, frequent and prolonged absences from Cambridge, and these gave the University cause to question his activities and to threaten, in 1587, to withhold his final degree. But Marlowe had strings to pull. A letter from the Privy Council with the overruling authority of, among others, Archbishop Whitgift, Sir Christopher Hatton, and Lord Burghley, explained in veiled hints the reason for these absences: Marlowe 'had done Her Majestie good service, and deserved to be rewarded for his faithfull dealinge'[3]. He probably went abroad —perhaps to visit the English Catholics at Rheims. Amidst much speculation one thing is clear: this 'good service' was not of the kind that is officially recorded and recognised.

[1] Thomas Beard, *Theatre of God's Judgements* (1597), ch. xxv
[2] See William Urry, 'Marlowe and Canterbury', *T.L.S.* (13th February 1964)
[3] Privy Council Register, xxix° Junij 1587; for a full documentation of Marlowe's life and death see J. Leslie Hotson, *The Death of Christopher Marlowe* (1925) and John Bakeless, *The Tragicall History of Christopher Marlowe* (Harvard, 1945)

A secret agent with an M.A. degree, Marlowe left Cambridge for London. There he consorted with playwrights, at one time sharing a room with Thomas Kyd, author of *The Spanish Tragedy*; quite possibly he associated also with the group of young intellectuals led by Sir Walter Raleigh. Although the facts of his life are largely unknown, its tenor is certain. Arrested once on a charge of homicide, bound over at another time to keep the peace, Marlowe emerges from contemporary legal documents as a rash and fearless quarreller. Mario Praz calls him a *libertin*, using the word to mean both 'freethinker' and, with its accumulated secondary meaning, 'man of loose morals'[1]. For the free-thinking there is ample evidence of surprising consistency. Richard Baines libelled Marlowe only a few days after the murder. The now famous libel accuses the dramatist of blaspheming the Bible and mocking the state, reporting him as having said:

> ... That the first beginning of Religion was only to keep men in awe ...
> ... That Christ was a bastard and his mother dishonest ...
> ... that all the new testament is filthily written ...

Whatever the company he came into, Baines continued, Marlowe persuaded its members to atheism,

> willing them not to be afeard of bugbears and hobgoblins, and utterly scorning both god and his ministers[2].

Marlowe sounds alternately like a perky undergraduate and like a man of plain common sense. But this is a twentieth-century view. To the Elizabethans, fearing for the sanctity of their church and the security of their state, these were 'monstruous opinions', menacing heresies. A warrant was issued for Marlowe's arrest, on evidence supplied perhaps by his former friend Kyd. Kyd himself had been arrested, accused of inciting mob violence and race riots against the Flemish protestants who were then settling in England. Under torture he broke down, and in two letters to Sir John Puckering, the Lord Keeper, he charged Marlowe with heresy and blasphemy.

Before the warrant could be executed Marlowe was killed. The inquest report tells of a squalid encounter in a Deptford tavern on 30 May 1593. Marlowe spent the day there with three 'gentlemen', talking and walking in the garden. But in the evening a quarrel was struck up over who should pay the bill, '*le recknynge*', and in the scuffle that followed Marlowe drew his dagger and wounded one of his companions. The man, Ingram Frizar, snatched the weapon and

> in defence of his life, with the dagger aforesaid of the value of 12d. gave the said Christopher then & there a mortal wound

[1] 'Christopher Marlowe', *E.S.*, XIII (1931)
[2] MS Harley 6648, ff. 185–6

over his right eye of the depth of two inches & of the width of one inch; of which mortal wound the aforesaid Christopher Morley then & there instantly died.[1]

The coroner's account puts a good face on the matter. Yet Ingram Frizar and one, if not both, of his accomplices had connections in some uncertain way with the secret service. Their past histories, and the speed with which, one month later, Frizar was granted a free pardon for the murder, suggest that the 'recknynge' settled in the Deptford tavern was an old score, dating perhaps as far back as Marlowe's Cambridge and Secret Service days.

Marlowe's contemporaries accepted the story of the brawl, but only one seems to have known its ostensible cause. Shakespeare's reference to Marlowe's death serves as an epitaph on his life, the brief life of his most brilliant colleague whose achievement, in five years, is second only to Shakespeare's own:

> A great reckoning in a little room
> *As You Like It*, III.iii, 11.

THE PLAY

THE DATE

Marlowe's reputation rests on four great plays: *Tamburlaine* (in two parts), 1587–8; *The Jew of Malta*, 1590; *Edward II*, 1592; and *Dr. Faustus*. At Cambridge Marlowe wrote a few translations of Latin poets and perhaps also the early play *Dido Queen of Carthage* which has only recently received[2] the attention it merits for its compound of high tragedy and wry comedy. The later (1590–93) *Massacre at Paris*, journalistic and popular, has been justly neglected. Unfinished at Marlowe's death was *Hero and Leander*, an epic poem of great delight, promising for its author, had he lived, certainty of success in a new field.

The proud-paced verse of *Tamburlaine* stormed the English stage. For his first public theme Marlowe took the story of a peasant warrior whose aspiring mind impelled him to conquest. Over a map of the world, drawn with detailed accuracy from Ortelius' *Theatrum Orbis Terrarum*, Marlowe played 'a great game of chess, with kings and conquerors for pieces'.[3] Barabas, protagonist of *The Jew of Malta*, is the reverse of Tamburlaine; schemes of grandeur delight him less

---

[1] Chancery Miscellanea, Bundle 64, File 8, No. 2416 (translated from the Latin)
[2] from J. B. Steane, *Marlowe: a critical study* (1964)
[3] Ethel Seaton, 'Marlowe's Map', *E & S*, X (1924), p. 35

than grotesquely comic revenge plots to poison a whole convent of nuns. Far from striding across the known world in the majesty of power, he huddles in his counting-house, accumulating from all quarters of the globe 'Infinite riches in a little room'. King Edward lacks even this ambition, longing only for the 'nook or corner' which all England cannot afford where he may indulge his love for Gaveston. 'Marlowe's mighty line' (the description is Ben Jonson's[1]) is restrained in *Edward II*, but what seems like a loss in energy is compensated by a gain in human feeling.

Not one of Marlowe's plays can be dated with any precision, but none presents so great a problem here as *Dr. Faustus*. The critic's immediate impulse is to place it between *Tamburlaine* and *The Jew of Malta* – i.e. about 1589. The soaring splendour of the verse strongly resembles that of *Tamburlaine* but marks an advance on the early play in its irony, its more critical detachment. The fragmentary text of *Dr. Faustus* bears no signs of the firmer grasp of construction and characterization that is felt in *Edward II*; apart from Mephostophilis' one moment (I.iii) the spotlight focuses on the single figure of Faustus, leaving the rest of the *dramatis personae* in the shadows. Faustus too, in his aspect of Renaissance superman bent on subduing the world to his will, is more closely akin to Tamburlaine than to either of the smaller natures, Barabas and Edward. Taken in this order, the four plays have an intrinsic coherence, illustrating (though Marlowe's conscious mind probably admitted no such intention) 'the progressive stages in the downfall of the humanist ideal'[2].

Against this internal evidence for an early date must be balanced one external fact. There is no edition, record, or specific mention of Marlowe's source (see below) before 1592. *Dr. Faustus* must be Marlowe's last play, the successor to *Edward II*, unless the dramatist had access, somehow or other, to *EFB* either in manuscript or else in an unrecorded edition prior to the one late in 1592. That there was such an edition, now wholly lost, is generally accepted: two publishers disputed ownership of the copyright in December 1592, and the extant text claims to contain 'imperfect matter amended'. Greg, however, is fairly certain that the first edition antedates the second by a matter of months only[3].

In the battle to fix an early date for the play, further ammunition has been brought from other writings, both dramatic and nondramatic. Kocher, firing at the base of the late-date argument, claims an edition of *EFB* before 1590.[4] Muir and Zimansky both hear

[1] line 30 of his memorial verses to Shakespeare, published in the First Folio
[2] M. M. Mahood, 'Marlowe's Heroes', *Poetry and Humanism* (1950), p. 85
[3] Greg, pp. 1–6
[4] 'The English *Faust Book* and the Date of Marlowe's *Faustus*', *M.L.N.*, LV (1940); and 'The Early Date for Marlowe's *Faustus*', *M.L.N.*, LVIII (1943)

echoes of *Dr. Faustus* in other plays. The former points out simi-
larities between Faustus' last soliloquy and a passage in *Looking
Glass for London* by Lodge and Greene which must have been
written before August 1591,[1] while the latter offers similar evidence
from *A Knack to Know A Knave*, acted in June 1592.[2]

The witness of the play itself, backed by the circumstantial
evidence brought by scholars, seems to me to outweigh the solitary
fact in the opposite scale. But the verdict is by no means conclusive,
and the case is still proceeding.

THE SOURCE

THE
HISTORIE
of the damnable
life, and deserved death of
Doctor Iohn Faustus,
Newly imprinted, and in conveni-
ent places imperfect matter amended.
according to the true Copie printed
at Franckfort, *and translated into
English by* P. F. *Gent*.[3]

Stories of witchcraft and enchantment, wandering loose in men's
minds, attached themselves in the early sixteenth century to a real-
life Georg or Johannes Faustus, scholar and reputed magician of no
fixed abode. After this man's death – which gave rise to the most
fantastic story of all – his fabled doings' were assembled in a 'bio-
graphy' published in Frankfurt in 1587. The book caught the eye of
an Englishman and, translated, was an immediate success. Nothing,
not even the name, is known of the translator, P. F. *Gent*. Whoever
he was, P. F. shared the German author's staunchly protestant out-
look. At some time, however, he must have toured Italy, and because
of his efforts to turn the pious jestbook into a Blue Guide we can be
certain that Marlowe used the English translation and not the German
original. The German, for instance, makes only passing reference to
Venice, whereas P. F. remarks the Piazza San Marco and 'the sumptuous Church standing therein called Saint *Markes*; how all the
pavement was set with coloured stones, and all the Roode or loft of

[1] 'The Chronology of Marlowe's Plays', *Proceedings of the Leeds Philosophical
and Literary Society*, V (1943); and see below p. xvii
[2] 'Marlowe's *Faustus*: the Date Again', *P.Q.*, XLI (1962)
[3] British Museum, C.27.b.43.

the Church double gilded over' (ch. xxii). Marlowe copies – and adds a further detail:

> In midst of which a sumptuous temple stands,
> That threats the stars with her aspiring top,
> Whose frame is paved with sundry coloured stones,
> And roofed aloft with curious work in gold.
>   III.i, 17–20

But the 'aspiring top'– unless Marlowe can be thinking of the adjacent campanile – exists only in the dramatist's imagination.

More intelligent than either of his predecessors, Marlowe had more respect for his hero. No longer the conjuror and calendar-maker of the source, this Faustus is a scholar of distinction. Marlowe's own learning went to the creation of his protagonist, and the verse of the play is heavily encrusted with references to texts that the Cambridge undergraduate must have studied. Professor Brockbank has noted the similarity, not only in name, of Marlowe's Faustus and the Manichean bishop who appeared to St Augustine.[1]

In the comic pope and anti-pope scene (III.i) can be traced the vestiges of history, and for these John Foxe's *Actes and Monuments*[2] was the source. Alexander III, pope from 1159 until 1181, encountered a rival in Victor IV who was installed by the Emperor Frederick Barbarossa; after long disputes Alexander won his cause and compelled Frederick to kneel at his feet:

> The proud pope setting his foot upon the emperors necke, said the verse of the psalms: *Super aspidem et basilicum ambulabis, et conculcabis leonem et draconem* . . . To whome the emperor answering again, said: *Non tibi sed Petro* . . . The pope again: *Et mihi et Petro.*
>
>   5th ed. (1596), p. 183

Historical fact has been confused, even violated. But this is of small importance.

THE TEXT

Two early texts, published within a few years of each other yet differing widely, make *Dr. Faustus* a most complicated editorial problem. The version now referred to as the A Text appeared in 1604 and was reprinted, each time with a few minor changes, in 1609 and 1611. In 1616 another version, the B Text, was published; this was reprinted five times before 1633. The second (1619) edition of this text tells us that it is 'With new Additions'–a piece of informa-

---

[1] J. P. Brockbank, *Marlowe: 'Dr Faustus,'* (1962), pp. 13-15
[2] popularly known as Foxe's *Book of Martyrs* (first English version 1563)

tion that ought to have been given three years earlier. For a long time it was thought that A was the more original and that the new parts of B (III.i, 90 ff.; ii; IV.i–vi; vii, 32 ff.; V.ii, 1–23, 85–130; iii) were the 'adicyones' for which Henslowe paid £4 to a couple of his hack writers, Bird and Rowley, in 1602.[1] Modern bibliographical study, however, has worked to reverse these views. Leo Kirschbaum in 1946 demonstrated that A bears all the stigmata of a reported text – a text assembled by an actor, perhaps, from memory.[2] Greg, already at work on his *Parallel Texts*, followed up this line of thought to argue that A is indeed a reported, shortened version of the play represented by B; that B was set up in different parts from a copy of A3 (1611) alone, from A3 corrected by the author's manuscript, and from MS. alone; and that the additional writing had been there from the beginning. To account for the occasional superiority of A (most notably at V.i, 25–33) he postulated a revision of the play by Marlowe which found its way into the theatrical prompt-book but not into the original MS.

The monumental structure of Greg's argument commands admiration but inhibits further building on the same site. My own view is that the MS. behind the B Text came from the playhouse and incorporated the Bird–Rowley additions in its third and fourth acts at least. The extra lines in V.ii may have been part of this later revision or, since they demand more elaborate staging (a balcony, the gaping hell-mouth, and a celestial throne) they may have been dropped from the production reported by A, which was in every way less spectacular. Such a theory gives less weight than Greg attributes to the B Text, while still maintaining its general authority.

Some kind of MS., certainly, was used in preparing the B Text, but the detailed stage directions which this apparently provided suggest rather a theatrical book than the author's foul papers. Embedded in the Latin of Faustus' invocation (I.iii, 19) is the English word *Dragon*; its position in the text suggests that the word must have been scrawled in the margin and misunderstood by an already bemused compositor who printed it into the text. Restoring it as a stage direction Boas, followed by Greg, looks to *EFB* for an explanation and finds that, while Faustus was conjuring, 'over his head hanged hovering in the ayre a mighty Dragon' (ch. ii). The same, they infer, must have happened on the stage. But what sort of producer would draw the attention away from Faustus at such a moment? That which is effective in a narrative is not always dramatically viable. An alternative suggestion was put forward by Kirschbaum[3] who saw the direction as anticipatory, a warning to the props

[1] *Henslowe's Diary*, ed. Foakes and Rickert (1961), p. 206
[2] 'The Good and Bad Quartos of *Dr. Faustus*', *The Library*, XXVI (1945–6)
[3] 'Mephostophilis and the lost "Dragon" ', *R.E.S.*, XVIII (1942)

man to have his dragon ready so that it could pop up through the trapdoor a few lines later. In his haste, Faustus forgets to stipulate that the devil should appear to him in some pleasing shape, and the titlepages of all the B quartos carry a woodcut showing a genial Faustus looking askance at what is surely an emergent dragon.[1] A stage direction of this kind would never appear in an author's MS. Similarly the direction Enter FAUSTUS *with the false head* (IV.iii, 37) suggests, by the use of the definite article, a writer familiar with the company's property resources. Greg admits that this, like the direction *Enter Piramus with the Asse Head*[2] reads as though it were written by some theatrical hand. Again, Robin in the comic scenes is consistently referred to in directions and speech headings as *Clown*; Lancelot Gobbo in *The Merchant of Venice* is treated in the same way, and this is usually ascribed to a stage book-keeper. These directions in *Dr. Faustus*, incidentally, seem to have led Greg to think of Robin as the Clown of I.iv. Probably the same actor played both parts, but Robin is as different from the earlier Clown as the smart-alec comedian of the television is from the red-nosed comic man of the old Music Hall.

Greg detects the hand of an 'editor' preparing B's text for publication, censoring anything that might be accounted blasphemous under the 1606 Act of Abuses. Thus Faustus' line 'O I'll leap up to my God' (V.ii, 143) becomes 'O I'll leap up to heaven', and the following line, 'See, see where Christ's blood streams in the firmament', is omitted completely. Censorship of this kind would be more appropriate for a stage performance, since the text could be printed at any time after the acting version had been 'allowed'. Minor variants in the B Text become suspect once the hand of an 'editor' is admitted, and I view this man with more suspicion than Greg does. At I.i, 131 A reads 'That yearly stuffs old Phillip's treasury'; B alters *stuffs* to *stuff'd*. Greg sees a compositor's error, but I agree with Boas in suggesting an editor's dutiful correction to the past tense after Philip of Spain's death in 1598. More substantial is the variance between A and B at the end of I.ii where I detect an amateur poet turning prose into verse (see note p. 14).

The theory of prompt-book revision is most suspicious. I find it hard to believe that Marlowe wrote so very badly when drafting the Scholars' reactions to Helen (see note p. 77). These lines in A's version must be considered along with another passage, again found only in A. Greg rejects certain parts of A as being actors' interpolations which would inevitably creep into a reported text. I agree with the principle but disagree over the choice of passages to be consigned

[1] The titlepage of Q 1624 has been used for this edition since the other quartos are in some way mutilated.
[2] In the Folio text of *A Midsummer Night's Dream*, III.i.

to the oblivion of an appendix. Act I scene iv needs closer examination. I have, to begin with, retained the 'French crowns' joke which Greg discarded on false historical grounds (see lines 26–9 and note), but I have followed his example in throwing out two mildly obscene passages for which I can find no justification (see note p. 20). The 'kill devil' lines (35–9) are another matter. Greg refuses to allow them into his text because, he argues, they were filched from *A Looking Glass for London* whose Clown boasts

> Then may I count myselfe I thinke a tall man, that am able to kill a divell. Now who dare deale with me in the parish, or what wench in *Ninivie* will not love me, when they say, there goes he that beate the divell.

1732–5

Muir pointed out resemblances between Faustus' last soliloquy and the Usurer's despair in this play[1]; in fact *A Looking Glass* and its relationship to *Dr. Faustus* will bear closer inspection than either Muir or Greg has been able to give it. In the A Text the First Scholar remarks:

> Since we have seen the pride of Nature's works,
> And only paragon of excellence . . . V.i, 30–31

In *A Looking Glass* we find the phrases 'pride of nature's excellence' (line 433) and 'gratious paragon of excellence' (line 1521). Either, even both, of these might have been arrived at independently, but taken in conjunction with the echoes of the last soliloquy and a few other minor resemblances to *Dr. Faustus*, they add up to fairly weighty evidence, not only for an early date to the play but also, more relevantly here, for the originality of some hitherto rejected parts of the A Text. We cannot discard the 'kill devil' lines and retain the First Scholar's comment unless we allow two-way traffic along this road.

Finally, what of the additional writing in the B Text? Greg's argument for the originality of the Bruno and Benvolio scenes hinges on one verbal parallel and one allusion. Echoes of *Dr. Faustus* are frequent in the anonymous *Taming of a Shrew* (printed 1594) and the lines from scene xv

> This angrie sword should rip thy hatefull chest,
> And hewd thee smaller then the Libian sands[2]

Greg takes as a repetition of Faustus' words

> And had you cut my body with your swords,
> Or hewed this flesh and bones as small as sand
> IV.iii, 73–4

---

[1] *Vid. sup.* p. xiii.   [2] The line derives directly from Catullus vii. 3: *'quam magnus numerus Libyssae harena'*.

It is, he freely admits, 'one of the least convincing of the parallels',[1] but he claims further substantiation for the case from a reference in *The Merry Wives of Windsor:*

> so soon as I came beyond Eton, they threw me off, from behind one of them, in a slough of mire; and set spurs and away, like three German devils, three Doctor Faustuses.
>
> IV.v, 53–6

This is tricky. The passage may refer to the action of IV.iv – though even here a certain doubt is permissible. It appears in one of the textually most bewildering scenes of *Merry Wives*[2] and is found in the Folio text of the play but not in the Bad Quarto of 1602. For this to be received as evidence Greg's hypothesis about the text of Shakespeare's play must also be accepted. Greg argues a revision of the play before the performance reported in Q1, but Pollard and Wilson suggest multiple revisions including one in 1604. On their hypothesis the passage might have got into the text between 1602 and 1604. Certainly the manuscript for IV. i–iv must have been written by a different hand from the rest of the play: the abbreviated form *I'll* is consistently spelt *I'le* except in this section (ff. E2ᵛ–F3) where *Il'e* is used.

The additions to Act V are less easy to discuss objectively; and in the absence of any external evidence the only criterion is in the ear of the reader. Boas and Greg can both hear Marlowe's voice in the first twenty-three lines of V.ii. There is one minor point. Instances of a regular verse line divided between two speakers, a striking feature of *Edward II*, are rare in *Dr. Faustus;* of the nine, five occur in obviously non-Marlovian scenes (III.i, 90, 123; IV.iii, 38; IV.iv, 12, 14) and the other four in these doubtful portions of V.ii (lines 7, 21, 99, 102). The whole nature of the play is changed by this addition. Without it we have the tragedy of an individual who wilfully seeks his own destruction; with it, *Dr. Faustus* is a more medieval play where man is a puppet manipulated by external powers.

The authorship of the play is as much in doubt as its text. The Bruno scenes, with their glibly versified violation of historical fact, show some of the characteristics of Rowley's work – and Rowley, moreover, had used the same source for his *When You See Me You Know Me*. Nashe has been convincingly presented as Marlowe's collaborator on the comic scenes.[3] But the man who wrote the Robin and Ralph scenes did not, I am sure, write the earlier comedy scenes with Wagner (I.ii and iv). Here the parody of the main plot is satirical,

[1] Greg, p. 28
[2] See E. K. Chambers, *William Shakespeare* (1930), i.425–8
[3] By Kocher, 'Nashe's Authorship of the Prose Scenes in *Faustus*', *M.L.Q.*, III (1942)

not farcical; an intelligence is at work, and I suspect it is Marlowe's own.

Whoever wrote the comic scenes, no one but Marlowe can take credit for the tragedy.

THE TRAGEDY

The Tragicall History
of
the life and death
of
DR. FAUSTUS

Boundless in its aspirations, unceasing in its compulsions, the Renaissance mind is the theme of all Marlowe's plays:

> Our souls, whose faculties can comprehend
> The wondrous architecture of the world,
> And measure every wandering planet's course,
> Still climbing after knowledge infinite,
> And always moving as the restless spheres,
> Will us to wear ourselves and never rest . . .
> 1 Tamburlaine, II.vii, 21–6

Dr. Faustus, although he is the first figure on the English stage who deserves to be called a character, is still less an individual than the epitome of Renaissance aspiration. He has all the divine discontent, the unwearied and unsatisfied striving after knowledge that marked the age in which Marlowe wrote. An age of exploration, its adventurers were not only the merchants and seamen who sailed round the world, but also the scientists, astronomers who surveyed the heavens with their 'optic glass', and those scholars who travelled in the realms of gold to bring back tales of a mighty race of gods and heroes in ancient Greece and Rome. The first soliloquy is 'no mere reckoning of accounts but an inventory of the Renaissance mind'[1]. Faustus is one of the new men. For him, as for Marlowe, lowly birth was no bar to a university education, and as he sits alone in his study reading from the Latin text books he is linked in a common language with scholars from Oxford, Cambridge and all over the civilized world. Rhetoric, jurisprudence and medicine have trained a mind apt for questioning, eager for learning, and reluctant to take on trust even the most elementary facts, let alone those hypotheses incapable of empirical proof. The Faustus who refuses to accept from Mephostophilis the evidence for hell's existence is true to type. His pitiful shortsightedness is all too evident, but there is also a determination to believe

[1] Harry Levin, *Christopher Marlowe: the Overreacher* (1954, 2nd ed. 1965), p. 134

only what he himself can prove. This has made him the distinguished scholar he is, the man whose triumphant cry '*sic probo*' has echoed his fame through the German universities. Men of Faustus' calibre were not unknown to Marlowe's age. They were valuable and they were dangerous. Sir Walter Raleigh and his friends, meeting together to discuss philosophy, to debate religion, and to gaze at the stars through Thomas Heriot's new telescope, attracted much popular and unwanted attention. They were accused of witchcraft and devil-worship. James VI, piously warning his Scottish subjects against the deceits of the devil, observed that those attracted to black magic were, more often than not, men

> having attained to a great perfection in learning, & yet remaining overbare (alas) of the spirit of regeneration and frutes thereof: finding all naturall things common, aswell to the stupid pedants as unto them, they assaie to vendicate unto them a greater name, by not onlie knowing the course of things heavenlie, but likewise to clim to the knowledge of things to come thereby.
> *Daemonologie* (Edinburgh, 1597), p. 10

The more man discovered about the universe and his place in it, the more imperative it became for Authority to stress the dangers inherent in the pursuit of knowledge. The wrath of the Almighty and the threat of eternal damnation were powerful deterrents.

When the play opens Faustus stands at the frontiers of knowledge. The whole of Renaissance learning is within his grasp, but on closer scrutiny of the parts the whole crumbles away and he is left with nothing but a handful of dust. Nothing in the great university curriculum can overcome the melancholy fact – 'Yet art thou still but Faustus, and a man' (I.i, 23). Faustus shares with Hamlet, equally a product of Wittenberg scepticism, this perception of man's paradoxical nature:

> What a piece of work is a man! how noble in reason! how infinite in faculties! . . . the beauty of the world, the paragon of animals! And yet, to me, what is this quintessence of dust?
> *Hamlet*, II.ii, 293–7

It is this that gives rise to the irony that is the characteristic mode of the play: Faustus begins by longing to be more than human; he ends by imploring metamorphosis into the sub-human. Incidental ironies have a sharp impact within this structure – as when Faustus seals his deed of blood with the last words of Christ on the cross: '*Consummatum est*' (II.i, 74). The impassioned appeal

> O Christ my saviour, my saviour,
> Help to save distressed Faustus' soul
> II.ii, 83–4

is answered by the emergence of the infernal trinity looking, as Steane comments, like 'the party bosses in a totalitarian state before one guilty of thought-crime.'[1] Certain words, frequently reiterated, carry an ambivalence that points to this initial paradox. Both *cunning* and *conceit* were at a semantic crossroads when Marlowe wrote. The translator of the Psalms could write, for the Authorized Version, 'If I forget thee, O Jerusalem, let my right hand forget her cunning' (Ps. 137) at much the same time as Bacon gave the definition 'We take cunning for a sinister and crooked wisdom'.[2] Marlowe plays delicately with both meanings, often balancing the older usage against the newer:

> Till, swollen with cunning, of a self-conceit.
>
> Prologue, line 20

Neither *cunning* nor *conceit*, however, has the force Marlowe can give to the simple word *man*. Faustus envisages a world of power and delight which 'Stretcheth as far as doth the mind of man' (I.i, 60). Human potential is set against human limitation in a single word. It is to redeem himself, by his own efforts, from this paradox that Faustus turns longing eyes on the magic books that will make him a 'mighty god' and ultimately damn him for ever.

Dr. Faustus is a tragedy of damnation. In his source Marlowe found the story of a scholar who gave his soul to the devil in return for twenty-four years of knowledge and pleasure. The rewards were miserably inadequate, and seem even more so in the play, where Faustus is shown as an approving spectator at a conventional masque of the Deadly Sins; as an astronaut circling the world; as a common illusionist entertaining at a Royal Command performance; and as a mystical greengrocer contenting a pregnant duchess with out-of-season grapes. An immortal soul is a heavy price to pay for such delights. There are some critics, most recently Warren D. Smith,[3] who claim that the trivialities of the middle parts of the play were planned by Marlowe, that the dramatist was bent on 'establishing evil, though terrible in consequence, as actually petty in nature.'[4] On such a reading one can trace the gradual deterioration in the character of the protagonist:

> From a proud philosopher, master of all human knowledge, to a trickster, to a slave of phantoms, to a cowering wretch: that is a brief sketch of the progress of Dr. Faustus.[5]

[1] *Marlowe*, p. 141
[2] *Essays*, 'Of Cunning'
[3] 'The Nature of Evil in *Dr. Faustus*', *M.L.R.*, LX (April, 1965)
[4] p. 171.
[5] Helen Gardner, 'The Tragedy of Damnation', *Elizabethan Drama*, ed. R. J. Kaufmann (New York, 1961), p. 321

But I am not at all convinced that the coherence which such a view demands is there in the play. What Marlowe wrote is easy enough to detect; what he planned, either to write himself or to be added by a collaborator, is mere conjecture.

In those parts of the play where Marlowe's hand is unmistakable, there is more than enough evidence for Faustus' damnation. To read it properly, however, we must concentrate on an aspect of the dramatist that is usually neglected.

Quarrelsome, violent, homosexual, a mocking atheist – this is the Marlowe of contemporary scandal and the one who is best known today. But before this came the holder of the Archbishop Parker scholarship, the Cambridge student of divinity. Whatever the older Marlowe made of his reading, the younger Marlowe (and a very few years separate the two) studied the theological texts in the library of Corpus Christi as avidly and earnestly as his Faustus promises to read Lucifer's presentation volume. Evidence of this is in Mephostophilis' account of the torments of deprivation:

> Think'st thou that I, who saw the face of God,
> And tasted the eternal joys of heaven,
> Am not tormented with ten thousand hells,
> In being deprived of everlasting bliss?
>   I.iii, 77–80

The words are not those of *EFB*, nor do they come from Marlowe's imagination; they are directly translated from the Latin of St. John Chrysostom (see note p. 19). Just before this Faustus, refusing to distinguish between the Christian hell and the pagan Elysium, proposes for himself an eternity among the Greek philosophers in the words of Averroes (see note p. 18). Marlowe the theologian has as great a part in this play as Marlowe the rebel. The theology is orthodox, but Marlowe's God is more long-suffering than the God of the Elizabethan church and continues to extend mercy and forgiveness to Faustus long after the traditional God would have turned away.

Faustus takes his first step along the primrose path when he sets material benefits before spiritual blessings. Contemplating magic, anticipating its rewards with Valdes and Cornelius, he promises himself all the glory and riches of the Renaissance world. From Mephostophilis he demands to 'live in all voluptuousness' (I.iii, 92). Even before he succumbs to the lure of magic, his mind has been tempted by thoughts of wealth: 'Be a physician Faustus, heap up gold' (I.i, 14). Yet although this obsession with luxury is a flaw in the nature of one dedicated to the search for knowledge, its seriousness must not be magnified until it obscures the real issues. In the first soliloquy Faustus rejects the study of law, leaving it to the 'mercenary drudge,

Who aims at nothing but external trash' (I.i, 34–5); all the gold that
the doctor can heap up will not reconcile him to the limitations of
medical skill, through whose aid he can restore only health, not
life. And when, in an early agony of indecision, he weighs the profit
and the loss, it is not riches that he puts into the opposite scale:

> Have not I made blind Homer sing to me
> Of Alexander's love, and Oenon's death?
> And hath not he, that built the walls of Thebes
> With ravishing sound of his melodious harp,
> Made music with my Mephostophilis?
>
> II.ii, 26–30

With the help of magic he has gained entry into another world, a
world, later to be incarnate in Helen of Troy, whose value far exceeds
the riches of all the Venetian argosies, Indian gold and Orient pearl.

The process of damnation begins with the signing of the pact.
Greg[1] noted that critics have paid strangely little attention to the
first article of the infernal contract: 'that Faustus may be a spirit in
form and substance' (II.i, 96). To the Elizabethans, *spirit* used in
this way could mean only 'devil', and by assuming diabolic nature
Faustus, in the eyes of the orthodox, would be instantly damned.
Lucifer and all the fallen angels were beyond the reach of God's
mercy; although God still had power to forgive, they lacked the
capacity to repent. Aquinas is the chief authority here, and his
doctrine, expounded in *Summa Theologica* i, 64, is echoed to the
letter in one of Donne's sermons:

> To those that fell, can appertain no reconciliation; no more then
> to those that die in their sins; for *Quod homini mors, Angelis
> casus;* The fall of the Angels wrought upon them, as the death of
> a man does upon him.
>
> *LXXX Sermons* (1640), p.9

To Lucifer, with his legalistic turn of mind, the contract is binding:

> Christ cannot save thy soul, for he is just;
> There's none but I have interest in the same.
>
> II.ii, 85–6

The Bad Angel is similarly insistent, telling Faustus flatly

> Thou art a spirit, God cannot pity thee.
> II.ii, 13

The play would have stopped at this point, so far as the tragic part is
concerned, had Faustus, the Good Angel, and Marlowe himself
shared Lucifer's opinion as to the irrevocability of the compact. But
there is still hope in the Good Angel's comforting 'Faustus repent,

[1] 'The Damnation of Faustus', *M.L.R.*, XLI (1946)

yet God will pity thee' (II.ii, 12). By signing the bond with its ominous first clause Faustus is not cut off from forgiveness. Yet the effects of his sin, in turning away from God, make it virtually impossible for him to accept the offered mercy. Repentance is all that is needed, yet to his dismay he finds 'My heart's so hardened I cannot repent' (II.ii, 18).

The devils are adept at pricking the bubbles of human self-glorification, and Faustus' pride is punctured in his first encounter with Mephostophilis. Soaring, as he thinks, to the height of his powers as 'conjuror laureate', he is jolted sharply back to earth by the fiend's casual admission that the conjuring was of no real import: 'I came now hither of mine own accord' (I.iii, 44). Hell's rewards are as the dead sea apples to Milton's fallen angels: mere ashes in his mouth. Repeated questioning of Mephostophilis brings no satisfaction; the devil can tell him only what he already knows and, forbidden to speak the praise of God, cannot give him the answer he wants to hear:

FAUSTUS   Now tell me who made the world?
MEPHOSTOPHILIS
I will not.   II.ii, 67–8

His pride dashed, Faustus becomes increasingly aware of the emptiness of his bargain and the reality of damnation. The pride with which this Renaissance superman scorned his human nature and aspired to become 'a mighty god' leads inevitably to its opposite, despair. And although God will forgive violation of the decalogue, will forgive, even, blasphemy against Christ, there are some sins on which He will have no mercy:

> whosoever speaketh against the Holy Ghost, it shall not be forgiven him, neither in this world, neither in the world to come.
> Matthew xii, 32

The precise nature of the sin against the Holy Ghost, not defined in the Gospel, has always exercised theologians; but Renaissance thinkers generally agreed that pride and despair, inextricably linked, must be so called. The 'Schoolmen', writes Donne, have noted certain sins

> which they have called sins against the Holy Ghost, because naturally they shut out those meanes by which the Holy Ghost might work upon us. The first couple is, *presumption* and *desperation*; for presumption takes away the fear of God, and desperation the love of God . . . And truly . . . To presume upon God, that God cannot damn me eternally in the next world, for a few half-houres in this . . . Or to despair, that God will not save me . . . al these are shrewd and slippery approaches towards the sin against the Holy Ghost.
> *LXXX Sermons*, pp. 349–50

The play ends where it began, in the solitude of Faustus' study. It is here that Faustus damns himself finally and irrevocably. He is never closer to repentance than in the moments after the Old Man's speech with its reassurance

> Yet, yet, thou hast an amiable soul,
> If sin by custom grow not into nature.
>   V.i, 40–41

The man who has abjured the Scriptures, forsaken God, trafficked with the devil, can still 'call for mercy, and avoid despair' (V.i, 61). But hell's present physical tortures terrify him more than the thought of future damnation, and instead of withstanding the momentary agony (as the Old Man will do later) he requests instead the comfort of

> That heavenly Helen, which I saw of late,
> Whose sweet embracings may extinguish clear
> Those thoughts that do dissuade me from my vow,
>   V.i, 90–92

Helen of Troy, twice passing over the stage, pausing for one brief moment yet speaking nothing, is the key figure in *Dr. Faustus*. For this Faustus has sold his soul. All the glory that was Greece was embodied, for the Renaissance, in this woman; her story was the story in brief of another world, superhuman and immortal. Helen's first appearance to the Scholars is no accident, no mere matter of a dramatist making double use of a bright idea. After their single scene at the beginning of the play (I.ii) the Scholars seem to have been forgotten; but this scene has shown them as men of moderate awareness, eminently sensible and a little humourless. Their comments (V.i, 25–31) on the apparition equip us to judge for ourselves when it is seen again. Helen is the 'only paragon of excellence' in the eyes of these sober men, and their ordinary understanding is 'Too simple ... to tell her praise'. The second appearance, attended by two Cupids and heralded, we must assume, by the music directed for the earlier entrance, has a ritual solemnity. This, and the formal ordering of Faustus' speech, marks the episode as what T. S. Eliot would have called a 'moment in and out of time'.[1] Faustus breaks the silence with the awed amazement of Marlowe's finest lines:

> Was this the face that launched a thousand ships,
> And burnt the topless towers of Ilium?
>   V.i, 96–7

Declaring his devotion, he is exalted to heroic stature and promises

[1] *Four Quartets*, 'Little Gidding'

vigorous action in verse of soaring energy which comes to rest at last on Helen's lips:

> And then return to Helen for a kiss.
>
> V.i, 108

The speech is a rapture of applause – for Helen herself, for the eternal beauty of form, for all the glory that defies and withstands the canker of Time. But it is more than this. As the delighted verse surges forward to praise what is lovely and enduring, an undertow drags back to remind us that this beauty brought destruction: a city was burnt, topless towers laid in the dust. In the stillness of a single couplet the two movements are balanced:

> Brighter art thou than flaming Jupiter,
> When he appeared to hapless Semele.
>
> V.i, 111–12

Semele, despite repeated warnings, persisted in her demands to see her lover in all his splendour. But the sight of Jupiter's divine majesty was greater than mortal eyes could bear to look upon, and the 'hapless Semele' was consumed by the glory. Helen has all of Jupiter's terrible burning beauty – and Faustus is damned by the vision. This is no mere fancy of Marlowe's, powerful though such a fancy would be. That which appears as Helen is no more the woman herself than the apparition which so pleased the German Emperor was indeed Alexander. Faustus sees a spirit, a devil, in the form of Helen and, forgetful of his own admonitions to the Emperor, he speaks to it, touches it. Helen's lips 'suck forth' his soul in more than metaphor. The kiss signals the ultimate sin, demoniality, the bodily intercourse with spirits.[1] Now the Old Man gives up hope of saving Faustus; the Good Angel leaves him. After such knowledge there is no forgiveness.

The last soliloquy reverses the first. The proud scholar who had fretted at the restrictions imposed by the human condition and longed for the immortality of a god, now seeks to avoid an eternity of damnation. Like a trapped animal he lashes out against the mesh he has woven for himself, and becomes more entangled. To be physically absorbed by the elements, to be 'a creature wanting soul', 'some brutish beast', even, at the last, to be no more than 'little water drops'– this is the final hope of the pride of Wittenberg. Time is the dominant in this speech. The measured regularity of the opening gives way to a frantic tugging in two directions as Faustus suffers the opposing forces of Christ and Lucifer:

> O I'll leap up to my God! Who pulls me down?
>
> V.ii, 143

---

[1] First pointed out by Greg in the essay referred to above

The pace and the passion increase as the clock strikes relentlessly, and the second half-hour passes more quickly than the first. We are agonizingly aware of the last minutes of Faustus' life, trickling through the hour-glass with what seems like ever-increasing speed. But as each grain falls, bringing Faustus closer to his terrible end, we become more and more conscious of the deserts of vast eternity and damnation that open up beyond death. When Macbeth or Lear dies the tragedy is ended with a final harmonious chord, but the discords of Faustus' last lines cannot be resolved.

The Epilogue, with its cosy smugness, is bitterly inadequate. Leo Kirschbaum has said that, whatever Marlowe's own beliefs, 'there is no more obvious Christian document in all Elizabethan drama than *Doctor Faustus*'.[1] Yet Christianity has few positives in this play. The Good Angel with his celestial throne comes from a child's picture-book of heaven, and is nothing like as telling as Mephostophilis' cry of despair and deprivation. Marlowe's play demonstrates the fearful consequences of violating the Christian ethic, and for this it may be called a Christian document. But Marlowe's sympathies (if the energy of the verse means anything at all) are for the rebel, the man who is impeded in his pursuit of science, who is frustrated in his efforts to assert his individuality. The first three lines of the Epilogue lamenting Faustus' fall are in Marlowe's most assured manner:

> Cut is the branch that might have grown full straight,
> And burned is Apollo's laurel bough,
> That sometime grew within this learned man.

The rest is pious moralizing, lapsing into the alliteration ('fiendful fortune') of a by-gone age, and snapping the book shut with a tidy rhymed couplet. The vitality is lost, and with it the respect; this is mere lip-service to a distasteful yet ineluctable morality.

[1] 'Marlowe's Faustus: A Reconsideration', *R.E.S.*, XIX (1943), p. 229

FURTHER READING

Bradbrook, M. C.,	'Marlowe's *Dr. Faustus* and the Eldritch Tradition', *Essays on Shakespeare and Elizabethan Drama in Honour of Hardin Craig*, ed. R. Hosley (1963)
Brockbank, J. P.,	*Marlowe: Dr. Faustus* (1962)
Brooke, Nicholas,	'The Moral Tragedy of Doctor Faustus', *Cambridge Journal*, v.11 (1952)
Ellis Fermor, Una,	*Christopher Marlowe* (1927)
Gardner, Helen,	'The Tragedy of Damnation', *Elizabethan Drama*, ed. R. J. Kaufmann (New York, 1961)
Greg, W. W.,	'The Damnation of Faustus', *M.L.R.*, XLI (1946)
Hotson, J. L.,	*The Death of Christopher Marlowe* (1925)
Knights, L. C.,	'The Strange Case of Christopher Marlowe', *Further Explorations* (1965)
Kocher, Paul H.,	*Christopher Marlowe* (Chapel Hill, 1946)
Levin, Harry,	*The Overreacher* (1954)
Mahood, M. M.,	'Marlowe's Heroes', *Poetry and Humanism* (1950)
Maxwell, J. C.,	'The Sin of Faustus', *The Wind and the Rain*, IV (1947)
Morris, Brian (ed.),	*Christopher Marlowe, Mermaid Critical Commentaries* (1968)
Praz, Mario,	'Christopher Marlowe', *E.S.*, XIII (1931)
Smith, James,	'Marlowe's *Dr. Faustus* , *Scrutiny*, VIII.i (1939)
Steane, J. B.,	*Marlowe: a critical study* (1964)
Wilson, F. P.,	*Marlowe and the Early Shakespeare* (1953)

The Tragicall Histoɪ
of the Life and Death
of Doctor FAVSTVS.

With new Additions.

Written by *Ch. Mar.*

Printed at London for *Iohn Wright*, and are to be fold at his
fhop without Newgate, 1624.

THE PRESENT EDITION

B1 (1616) has been taken as the basis of this new edition published in the New Mermaid series, but the authority of the A text is such that in many cases I have preferred its readings to B's. Significant departures from the B text are noted at the foot of the relevant page. As a general rule these notes are printed above the line, together with simple explanations of verbal difficulties. More detailed and leisured notes are printed below the line.

Chorus
Dr. John Faustus
Wagner, *his servant, a student*
Valdes, ⎱
Cornelius, ⎰ *his friends, magicians*
Three Scholars, *students under* Faustus
An Old Man

Pope Adrian
Raymond, *King of Hungary*
Bruno, *the rival pope*
Cardinals of France *and* Padua
The Archbishop of Rheims

Charles V, *Emperor of Germany*
Martino, ⎱
Frederick, ⎬*knights at the Emperor's court*
Benvolio, ⎰
Duke of Saxony

Duke of Vanholt
Duchess of Vanholt

Robin, *also called the* Clown
Dick
A Vintner
A Horse-courser
A Carter
The Hostess *at an inn*

The Good Angel
The Bad Angel
Mephostophilis
Lucifer
Belzebub
Spirits *presenting* The Seven Deadly Sins
                    Alexander the Great
                    Alexander's Paramour
                    Darius, *King of Persia*
                    Helen of Troy

Devils, Bishops, Monks, Soldiers *and* Attendants]

3

PROLOGUE

Enter CHORUS

CHORUS

Not marching in the fields of Thrasimene,
Where Mars did mate the warlike Carthagens,
Nor sporting in the dalliance of love
In courts of kings, where state is overturned,
Nor in the pomp of proud audacious deeds,   5
Intends our Muse to vaunt his heavenly verse:
Only this, Gentles – we must now perform
The form of Faustus' fortunes, good or bad.
And now to patient judgements we appeal,
And speak for Faustus in his infancy.   10
Now is he born, of parents base of stock,
In Germany, within a town called Rhode:
At riper years to Wittenberg he went,
Whereas his kinsmen chiefly brought him up;
So much he profits in divinity,   15
The fruitful plot of scholarism graced,
That shortly he was graced with doctor's name,

---

12 *Rhode* ed. (Rhodes Qq) Roda, since 1922 Stadtroda, in central
Germany
14 *Whereas* where
16 A (*not in* B) A credit to the rich academic discipline
17 *graced* At Cambridge a new Doctor of Divinity was enrolled in
the Book of Grace

Prologue 1–6
The Prologue speaks of plays already performed, but it is not clear
whether these were written by Marlowe or, more generally, are part of
the company's repertoire. In either case there is no trace of the first,
showing the victory of the Carthaginians under Hannibal at Lake
Trasimene (217 B.C.) If Marlowe's own plays are meant, ll.3–4 must
refer to *Edward II* and 1.5 to *Tamburlaine*. A masculine Muse (1.6) is
unusual but not unknown (*cf*. 'Lycidas', 19–21); yet Shakespeare, com-
paring himself with 'that Muse Stirred by a painted beauty to his verse',
(Sonnet XXI), clearly alludes to a rival poet. It seems to me that 'Muse'
here means simply 'Poet' and that the Chorus is speaking on behalf of
the actors.
13 *Wittenberg* Hamlet's university, and Luther's; the home of scepticism.
But this Wittenberg is, in all outward appearances, Marlowe's Cambridge.

Excelling all, whose sweet delight disputes
In th' heavenly matters of theology.
Till, swollen with cunning, of a self-conceit,   20
His waxen wings did mount above his reach,
And, melting, heavens conspired his overthrow:
For, falling to a devilish exercise,
And glutted now with learning's golden gifts,
He surfeits upon cursed necromancy: 25
Nothing so sweet as magic is to him,
Which he prefers before his chiefest bliss:
And this the man that in his study sits.

Exit

18 *whose sweet delight disputes* A (and sweetly can dispute B) whose
    great pleasure is in argument
20 *cunning* knowledge; usually knowledge misapplied;
    self-conceit pride in his own abilities
21–2 Icarus flew too near the sun on wings of wax; they melted and
    he fell into the sea
27 *chiefest bliss* i.e. hope of salvation

Act I, Scene i

FAUSTUS *in his study*

FAUSTUS

Settle thy studies, Faustus, and begin
To sound the depth of that thou wilt profess;
Having commenced, be a divine in show,
Yet level at the end of every art,
And live and die in Aristotle's works.
Sweet *Analytics*, 'tis thou hast ravished me:
Bene disserere est finis logices.
Is to dispute well logic's chiefest end?
Affords this art no greater miracle?
Then read no more, thou hast attained that end;
A greater subject fitteth Faustus' wit.
Bid *on kai me on* farewell; Galen come:
Seeing, *ubi desinit philosophus, ibi incipit medicus.*

2 *profess* specialize in, study and teach
3 *commenced* graduated; a Cambridge term;
   in show in appearance; show that you are indeed a student of theology
4 Consider the purpose of every discipline
12 *on kai me on* being and not being
13 Since the doctor starts where the philosopher leaves off; Aristotle,
   de sensu, 436a

1–36 Jump has pointed out that for the first part of Faustus' soliloquy
Marlowe seems to owe a debt to Lyly:
> Philosophie, Phisicke, Divinitie, shal be my studie. O ye hidden
> secrets of Nature, the expresse image of morall vertues, the equall
> balaunce of Justice, the medicines to heale all diseases, how they
> beginne to delyght me. The *Axiomaes* of *Aristotle,* the *Maxims* of
> *Justinian,* the *Aphorismes* of *Galen,* have sodaynelye made such a
> breache into my minde that I seeme onely to desire them which did
> onely earst detest them.
>   *Euphues* (1579), ed. Bond, i,241
5–7 Aristotle had been the dominant figure in the university curriculum
since the thirteenth century, but in Marlowe's day his supremacy was
challenged by Petrus Ramus (1515–72) whose ideas were defended in
Cambridge by William Temple. *Analytics* is the name give to two of
Aristotle's works on the nature of proof in argument, but the definition
of logic in 1.7 comes in fact from Ramus' *Dialecticae.* Ramus, his ideas
and his violent death, are displayed in Marlowe's *Massacre at Paris.*
12 *on kai me on* Bullen (Oncaymaeon A₁; Oeconomy A₂, ₃, B) The later
A texts were trying to make sense out of A₁'s apparent gibberish which
Bullen recognized as a transliteration of Aristotle's Greek phrase.

Be a physician Faustus, heap up gold,
And be eternized for some wondrous cure.   15
Summum bonum medicinae sanitas:
The end of physic is our body's health.
Why Faustus, hast thou not attained that end?
Is not thy common talk sound aphorisms?
Are not thy bills hung up as monuments,   20
Whereby whole cities have escaped the plague,
And thousand desperate maladies been cured?
Yet art thou still but Faustus, and a man.
Couldst thou make men to live eternally,
Or, being dead, raise them to life again,   25
Then this profession were to be esteemed.
Physic farewell! Where is Justinian?
Si una eademque res legatur duobus,
Alter rem, alter valorem rei etc.
A petty case of paltry legacies!   30
Exhereditare filium non potest pater nisi ...
Such is the subject of the Institute,
And universal body of the law.
This study fits a mercenary drudge,
Who aims at nothing but external trash,   35
Too servile and illiberal for me.
When all is done, divinity is best:
Jerome's Bible Faustus, view it well:
Stipendium peccati mors est: ha! *Stipendium, etc*
The reward of sin is death? That's hard.   40

15 *eternized* immortalized
16 Aristotle, *Nicomachean Ethics*, 1094.a.8
19 *aphorisms* medical precepts; after the *Aphorisms* of Hippocrates
20 *bills* prescriptions
28–9 If one and the same thing is bequeathed to two persons, one
   should have the thing itself, the other the value of the thing;
   Justinian, *Institutes*, ii,20
31 A father cannot disinherit his son unless ...; Justinian, ii,13
38 *Jerome's Bible* the Vulgate, prepared mainly by St Jerome; but
   the texts Faustus quotes are not in the words of the Vulgate
39 Romans, vi, 23

---

14 *heap up gold* The association of gold and the medical profession is an
   old one; Shakespeare mentions the use of gold for 'Preserving life in
   med'cine potable' (2 *Henry IV*, IV.v, 162). Faustus, however, is thinking of the profit to be gained – like Chaucer's Physician in *The Canterbury Tales*:
       For gold in phisik is a cordial,
       Therefore he lovede gold in special
                       Prologue, 444–5

Si peccasse negamus, fallimur, et nulla est in nobis veritas:
If we say that we have no sin, we deceive ourselves, and there
is no truth in us. Why then, belike, we must sin, and so con-
sequently die.
Ay, we must die an everlasting death.   45
What doctrine call you this? *Che sarà, sarà:*
What will be, shall be. Divinity adieu!
These metaphysics of magicians,
And necromantic books are heavenly;
Lines, circles, signs, letters and characters!   50
Ay, these are those that Faustus most desires.
O what a world of profit and delight,
Of power, of honour, of omnipotence,
Is promised to the studious artisan!
All things that move between the quiet poles   55
Shall be at my command: emperors and kings,
Are but obeyed in their several provinces,
Nor can they raise the wind, or rend the clouds;
But his dominion that exceeds in this,
Stretcheth as far as doth the mind of man: 60
A sound magician is a mighty god;
Here Faustus, try thy brains to gain a deity.

Enter WAGNER

Wagner, commend me to my dearest friends,
The German Valdes and Cornelius,
Request them earnestly to visit me.   65
WAGNER
I will sir.

                                                                    Exit

FAUSTUS
Their conference will be a greater help to me,
Than all my labours, plod I ne'er so fast.

Enter the ANGEL *and* SPIRIT

41 I John, i, 8
48 *metaphysics* supernatural sciences
50 *signs* ed. (scenes A; *not in* B) (see note on I.iii, 8–13)
54 *artisan* craftsman
55 *quiet poles* the poles of the universe, quiet because unmoving
57 *several* respective
58 A (*not in* B)
59 *this* this art, magic
61 *a mighty god* A (a demi-god B)
62 *Faustus, try thy brains to gain* A (tire, my brains, to get B)
68 s.d. *Spirit* (see note on II.i, 96)

GOOD ANGEL

  O Faustus, lay that damned book aside,
  And gaze not on it lest it tempt thy soul,   70
  And heap God's heavy wrath upon thy head:
  Read, read the Scriptures; that is blasphemy.

BAD ANGEL

  Go forward Faustus in that famous art
  Wherein all nature's treasury is contained:
  Be thou on earth as Jove is in the sky,   75
  Lord and commander of these elements.

                                     Exeunt ANGELS

FAUSTUS

  How am I glutted with conceit of this!
  Shall I make spirits fetch me what I please?
  Resolve me of all ambiguities?
  Perform what desperate enterprise I will?   80
  I'll have them fly to India for gold;
  Ransack the ocean for orient pearl,
  And search all corners of the new-found-world
  For pleasant fruits, and princely delicates.
  I'll have them read me strange philosophy,   85
  And tell the secrets of all foreign kings:
  I'll have them wall all Germany with brass,
  And make swift Rhine, circle fair Wittenberg:
  I'll have them fill the public schools with silk,
  Wherewith the students shall be bravely clad.   90
  I'll levy soldiers with the coin they bring,
  And chase the Prince of Parma from our land,
  And reign sole king of all our provinces.
  Yea, stranger engines for the brunt of war,

77 *glutted with conceit* drunk with the thought
84 *delicates* delicacies
89 *public schools* university lecture rooms;
   silk Dyce (skill Qq). In Marlowe's day undergraduates were
   ordered to dress soberly
90 *bravely* smartly
92 *Prince of Parma* Spanish governor-general of the Netherlands,
   1579–92
94 *engines* machines;
   brunt assault

75 *Jove* The names of pagan deities were frequently attributed to the
   Christian God; there is special force in this, coming from the Bad
   Angel.
87 *wall . . . brass* Friar Bacon, in Greene's *Friar Bacon and Friar Bungay*
   (before 1592) intended to 'circle England round with brass' (ii,178)
   when his magic schemes reached fruition.

Than was the fiery keel at Antwerp's bridge,   95
I'll make my servile spirits to invent.
Come German Valdes and Cornelius,
And make me blest with your sage conference.

Enter VALDES *and* CORNELIUS

Valdes, sweet Valdes, and Cornelius!
Know that your words have won me at the last   100
To practise magic and concealed arts;
Yet not your words only, but mine own fantasy,
That will receive no object for my head,
But ruminates on necromantic skill.
Philosophy is odious and obscure;   105
Both law and physic are for petty wits;
Divinity is basest of the three,
Unpleasant, harsh, contemptible and vile.
'Tis magic, magic that hath ravished me.
Then gentle friends, aid me in this attempt,   110
And I, that have with concise syllogisms
Gravelled the pastors of the German church
And made the flowering pride of Wittenberg
Swarm to my problems, as th'infernal spirits
On sweet Musaeus when he came to hell,   115
Will be as cunning as Agrippa was,
Whose shadows made all Europe honour him.
VALDES
Faustus, these books, thy wit, and our experience
Shall make all nations to canonise us.

101 *concealed* occult
102–4 A (*not in* B) Not your advice alone, but my own imagination has
    won me to this, allowing me to think of nothing else while it con-
    templates the possibilities of black magic
107–8 A (*not in* B)
111 *concise syllogisms* A₁,₂ (subtle syllogisms A₃, B) trenchant argument
112 *Gravelled* confounded, perplexed
114 *problems* topics of scholarly debate

  95 A bridge across the Scheldt, constructed by the Duke of Parma in the
     blockade of Antwerp, was attacked and destroyed by a fire-ship in April
     1585.
 115 *Musaeus* A legendary pre-Homeric bard often confused (as perhaps here)
     with Orpheus: *Aeneid* vi,667–8 describes Musaeus in the Elysian fields
     and *Georgics* iv tells of spirits swarming round Orpheus in the Under-
     world.
116–7 Henry Cornelius Agrippa von Nettesheim (1486–1535), magician
     and necromancer, was famous for his reputed power of invoking shades
     of the dead.

As Indian Moors obey their Spanish lords   120
So shall the spirits of every element
Be always serviceable to us three;
Like lions shall they guard us when we please,
Like Almaine rutters with their horsemen's staves,
Or Lapland giants trotting by our sides;   125
Sometimes like women or unwedded maids,
Shadowing more beauty in their airy brows,
Than have the white breasts of the Queen of Love.
From Venice shall they drag huge argosies,
And from America the golden fleece,   130
That yearly stuffs old Philip's treasury,
If learned Faustus will be resolute.

FAUSTUS
Valdes, as resolute am I in this,
As thou to live, therefore object it not.

CORNELIUS
The miracles that magic will perform,   135
Will make thee vow to study nothing else.
He that is grounded in astrology,
Enriched with tongues, well seen in minerals,
Hath all the principles magic doth require:
Then doubt not Faustus but to be renowned,   140
And more frequented for this mystery,
Than heretofore the Delphian oracle.
The spirits tell me they can dry the sea,
And fetch the treasure of all foreign wrecks;
Yea, all the wealth that our forefathers hid,   145

120 *Moors* dark-skinned natives; here specifically American Indians
124 Like German cavalry with lances
129 *argosies* treasure ships
130–31 America, whose richness is compared to the golden fleece
   sought by Jason and the Argonauts, paid annual tribute to Philip
   of Spain
134 *object it not* don't raise such objections
137 *grounded in* well schooled in
138 *well seen in minerals* informed about the properties of minerals
141 More sought after for practising this art
142 *Delphian oracle* the oracle of Apollo at Delphi

---

125 *Lapland giants* On another occasion Marlowe refers to the inhabitants
   of the polar regions in this way: 'tall and sturdy men, Giants as big as
   hugy Polypheme'. (2 *Tamburlaine*, I.i, 37–8)
138 *tongues* Greek and Hebrew were desirable for those who would converse
   with spirits, but Latin was the recognized common language: 'Thou art
   a scholar: speak to it Horatio.' *Hamlet*, I.i, 42

Within the massy entrails of the earth:
Then tell me, Faustus, what shall we three want?

FAUSTUS

Nothing Cornelius! O this cheers my soul!
Come, show me some demonstrations magical,
That I may conjure in some lusty grove,   150
And have these joys in full possession.

VALDES

Then haste thee to some solitary grove,
And bear wise Bacon's and Abanus' works,
The Hebrew Psalter, and New Testament;
And whatsoever else is requisite,   155
We will inform thee ere our conference cease.

CORNELIUS

Valdes, first let him know the words of art,
And then, all other ceremonies learnt,
Faustus may try his cunning by himself.

VALDES

First I'll instruct thee in the rudiments,   160
And then wilt thou be perfecter than I.

FAUSTUS

Then come and dine with me, and after meat
We'll canvass every quiddity thereof:
For ere I sleep, I'll try what I can do:
This night I'll conjure though I die therefore.   165

                                                            Exeunt omnes

146 *massy* solid
150 *lusty* A₁ (little A₂,₃; bushy B)
163 *canvass every quiddity* explore every detail; *quiddity* is a scholastic
    term denoting the essence of a thing, that which makes it what it is

---

153-4 *wise Bacon's and Abanus' works* Roger Bacon (1214?–94), protagonist
    of Greene's *Friar Bacon and Friar Bungay*, was an Oxford philosopher
    popularly supposed to have dabbled in black magic. Abanus is perhaps
    Pietro d'Abano (?1250–1316), Italian humanist and physician, also
    believed to have been a conjuror. As well as the works of these two,
    which would supply formulae for incantation, Faustus would need
    certain Psalms (especially 22 and 51) and the opening words of St.
    John's Gospel for his conjuring.
160 *rudiments* 'all that which is called vulgarly the vertue of worde, herbe, &
    stone: which is used by unlawful charmes, without natural causes . . .
    such kinde of charmes as commonlie daft wives use'.
        James I, *Daemonologie* (Edinburgh, 1597), p.11

Act I, Scene ii

Enter two SCHOLARS

1 SCHOLAR

I wonder what's become of Faustus, that was wont to make
our schools ring with *sic probo*.

2 SCHOLAR

That shall we presently know; here comes his boy.

Enter WAGNER

1 SCHOLAR

How now sirra, where's thy master?

WAGNER

God in heaven knows.　　　　　　　　　　　　　　　　　5

2 SCHOLAR

Why, dost not thou know then?

WAGNER

Yes, I know, but that follows not.

1 SCHOLAR

Go to sirra, leave your jesting, and tell us where he is.

WAGNER

That follows not by force of argument, which you, being
licentiates, should stand upon, therefore acknowledge your　　10
error, and be attentive.

2 SCHOLAR

Then you will not tell us?

WAGNER

You are deceived, for I will tell you: yet if you were not
dunces, you would never ask me such a question. For is he

---

　2 *sic probo* I prove it thus; a term from scholastic disputation
　3 *presently* at once
10 *licentiates* graduates; holders of a degree permitting them to study
　　for higher (master's or doctor's) degrees

---

14 *dunces* blockheads. The followers of Duns Scotus were commonly known
　　as Dunses, but since it is Wagner who indulges in the characteristic
　　Scotist cavilling it seems likely that he applies the word to the scholars
　　in its modern sense.

not *corpus naturale*? And is not that *mobile*? Then wherefore   15
should you ask me such a question? But that I am by nature
phlegmatic, slow to wrath, and prone to lechery – to love, I
would say – it were not for you to come within forty foot
of the place of execution, although I do not doubt but to
see you both hanged the next sessions. Thus having tri-   20
umphed over you, I will set my countenance like a precisian,
and begin to speak thus: Truly my dear brethren, my master
is within at dinner, with Valdes and Cornelius, as this wine,
if it could speak, would inform your worships: and so the
Lord bless you, preserve you, and keep you, my dear   25
brethren.

                                                                Exit

1 SCHOLAR
    Nay then, I fear he is fallen into that damned art, for which
    they two are infamous through the world.
2 SCHOLAR
    Were he a stranger, and not allied to me, yet should I grieve
    for him. But come, let us go and inform the Rector, and   30
    see if he by his grave counsel can reclaim him.
1 SCHOLAR
    I fear me, nothing will reclaim him now.
2 SCHOLAR
    Yet let us see what we can do.   *Exeunt*

19 *place of execution* the dining room; Wagner continues to make
   comic capital out of the phrase
21 *precisian* Puritan
30 *Rector* Head of the university

---

15 *corpus . . . mobile* a natural body and as such capable of movement.
   Aristotle's *corpus naturale seu mobile* was the current scholastic definition
   of the subject matter of physics.
27–31 B prints these lines as verse, altering the first to read 'O Faustus, then
   I fear that which I have long suspected'. The flatness of the verse,
   coming at the end of a scene of fairly pithy prose, casts some doubt on
   B's authenticity; there is, moreover, no reason why the Scholar should
   have 'long suspected' Faustus of necromantic proclivities. See Introduction, p. xvi.

Act I, Scene iii

Thunder. Enter LUCIFER *and four* DEVILS *above.*
FAUSTUS *to them, with this speech*

FAUSTUS

Now that the gloomy shadow of the earth,
Longing to view Orion's drizzling look,
Leaps from th'antarctic world unto the sky,
And dims the welkin, with her pitchy breath:
Faustus, begin thine incantations,   5
And try if devils will obey thy hest,
Seeing thou hast prayed and sacrificed to them.
Within this circle is Jehovah's name,
Forward and backward anagrammatised:
Th'abbreviated names of holy saints,   10
Figures of every adjunct to the heavens,
And characters of signs and erring stars,
By which the spirits are enforced to rise:
Then fear not Faustus, but be resolute
And try the uttermost magic can perform.   15

s.d. *Thunder . . . above* B (*not in* A)
  2 *Orion's drizzling look* the rainy constellation of Orion
 11 *adjunct* heavenly body fixed to the firmament (see note on II.ii,
    35–66)
 12 *characters* symbols; *signs and erring stars* signs of the Zodiac and
    planets

---

  1 *shadow of the earth* A (shadow of the night B) 'the night also, is no other
    thing but the shadow of the earth', La Primaudaye, *The French Academie*,
    III, xxxvii
  3 Marlowe seems to have thought that night advances from the southern
    hemisphere.
  7 *prayed and sacrificed.* A period of prayer and sacrifice, a kind of spiritual
    preparation, was a pre-requisite for conjuring.
 8–13 Before he began his conjuring the magician would draw a circle
    round himself, inscribing on the periphery certain signs (of the zodiac,
    for instance) and the tetragrammaton, the four Hebrew letters of the
    Divine Name. This was not only part of the invocation; so long as the
    circle was unbroken and the magician stayed inside it, no evil spirit
    could harm him.

(*Thunder*)

Sint mihi dei Acherontis propitii, valeat numen triplex Jehovae;
ignei, aerii, aquatici, terreni spiritus salvete! Orientis princeps,
Belzebub inferni ardentis monarcha, et Demogorgon, propi-
tiamus vos, ut appareat, et surgat Mephostophilis.

(*Dragon*)

Quid tu moraris? Per Jehovam, Gehennam, et consecratam   20
aquam, quam nunc spargo; signumque crucis quod nunc facio;
et per vota nostra, ipse nunc surgat nobis dicatus Mephostophilis.

Enter *a* DEVIL

I charge thee to return, and change thy shape,
Thou art too ugly to attend on me:
Go and return an old Franciscan friar,   25
That holy shape becomes a devil best.   *Exit* DEVIL
I see there's virtue in my heavenly words!
Who would not be proficient in this art?
How pliant is this Mephostophilis,
Full of obedience and humility,   30

17 *terreni* ed. (*not in* Qq) Faustus would call the spirits of all four
    elements
18 *Belzebub* Marlowe's form of the name has been retained because
    at certain points (e.g. II.i, 12) this suits better with the metre than
    the more commonly used Hebraic Beëlzebub
19 s.d. *Dragon* (see Introduction, p. xv)
20 *Quid tu moraris* Ellis (quod tumeraris Qq)

23–4 The wary magician always stipulated from the beginning that
    a pleasing shape should be assumed

16–22 'May the gods of Acheron look with favour upon me. Away with
    the spirit of the three-fold Jehovah. Welcome, spirits of fire, air, water
    and earth. We ask your favour, O prince of the East, Belzebub, monarch
    of burning hell, and Demogorgon, that Mephostophilis may appear
    and rise. Why do you delay? By Jehovah, Gehenna, and the holy water
    which I now sprinkle, and the sign of the cross which I now form, and
    by our vows, may Mephostophilis himself now rise, compelled to obey
    us'.
      Rejecting the Christian Trinity, Faustus turns to the infernal counter-
part (the prince of the East is Lucifer–see Isaiah, xiv, 12) He hails the
spirits of the elements: 'they make them believe, that at the fall of
Lucifer, some spirits fell in the aire, some in the fire, some in the water,
some in the lande' (*Daemonologie*, p.20). The name of Mephostophilis
(Marlowe's spelling is retained) was not, it seems, known before the
Faustus story; A. E. Taylor, in a letter to *T.L.S.* (6th December 1917)
suggests it might be glossed as the Greek *me faustopheles* – no true friend
to Faustus. Many versions of invocations to the devil express similar
surprise and impatience at his delay, after which the conjuror redoubles
his efforts. The sign of the cross had a double function; a powerful
charm to overcome diabolic disobedience, it also protected the conjuror
from injury by any spirit that might appear.

Such is the force of magic and my spells.
Now Faustus, thou art conjuror laureate
That canst command great Mephostophilis.
Quin redis, Mephostophilis, fratris imagine!

Enter MEPHOSTOPHILIS

MEPHOSTOPHILIS
Now Faustus, what wouldst thou have me do?   35
FAUSTUS
I charge thee wait upon me whilst I live
To do whatever Faustus shall command:
Be it to make the moon drop from her sphere,
Or the ocean to overwhelm the world.
MEPHOSTOPHILIS
I am a servant to great Lucifer,   40
And may not follow thee without his leave;
No more than he commands, must we perform.
FAUSTUS
Did not he charge thee to appear to me?
MEPHOSTOPHILIS
No, I came now hither of mine own accord.
FAUSTUS
Did not my conjuring speeches raise thee? Speak!   45
MEPHOSTOPHILIS
That was the cause, but yet *per accidens*:
For when we hear one rack the name of God,
Abjure the Scriptures, and his saviour Christ,
We fly in hope to get his glorious soul;
Nor will we come unless he use such means,   50
Whereby he is in danger to be damned:
Therefore the shortest cut for conjuring
Is stoutly to abjure the Trinity,
And pray devoutly to the prince of hell.

32–4 A (*not in* B)
34 Why do you not return, Mephostophilis, in the likeness of a friar
46 *per accidens* as it appeared; what the conjuring represented was the
   real cause
47 *rack* violate
53 *the Trinity* A (all godliness B)

38–9 Faustus would share these powers with the enchanters of classical
   literature (see Kocher, p. 141).
44 What Kocher (p. 160) calls the 'doctrine of voluntary ascent' is fairly
   well established in witchcraft.
47 *rack* Jump notes 'torment by anagrammatizing', but Mephostophilis
   has just explained that this is not necessary. 'Take the name of the
   Lord in vain' might be a better interpretation.

FAUSTUS

So Faustus hath already done, and holds this principle: 55
There is no chief but only Belzebub,
To whom Faustus doth dedicate himself.
This word 'damnation' terrifies not him,
For he confounds hell in Elysium:
His ghost be with the old philosophers.   60
But leaving these vain trifles of men's souls,
Tell me, what is that Lucifer thy lord?

MEPHOSTOPHILIS

Arch-regent and commander of all spirits.

FAUSTUS

Was not that Lucifer an angel once?

MEPHOSTOPHILIS

Yes Faustus, and most dearly loved of God.   65

FAUSTUS

How comes it then that he is prince of devils?

MEPHOSTOPHILIS

O, by aspiring pride and insolence,
For which God threw him from the face of heaven.

FAUSTUS

And what are you that live with Lucifer?

MEPHOSTOPHILIS

Unhappy spirits that fell with Lucifer,   70
Conspired against our God with Lucifer,
And are for ever damned with Lucifer.

FAUSTUS

Where are you damned?

MEPHOSTOPHILIS

In hell.

FAUSTUS

How comes it then that thou art out of hell?   75

---

59 *confounds hell in Elysium* makes no distinction between the Christian
concept of hell and the pagan (Greek) notion of the after-life in Elysium.
Marlowe has already coupled the two: 'Hell and Elysium swarm with
ghosts of men' (1 *Tamburlaine*, V.ii, 403). Nashe may be referring to
either of these passages when he scorns the writers that 'thrust Elisium
into hell' (Preface to Greene's *Menaphon* (1589), ed. McKerrow, iii, 316).
60 *old philosophers* those who shared his disbelief in an eternity of punishment; the line seems to come from a saying of Averroes, '*sit anima mea
cum philosophis*' (*cf*. J. C. Maxwell, *N & Q*, CXIV (1949), 334–5; J. M.
Steadman, *N & Q*, CCVII (1962), 327–9.)

MEPHOSTOPHILIS

Why this is hell, nor am I out of it.
Think'st thou that I, who saw the face of God,
And tasted the eternal joys of heaven,
Am not tormented with ten thousand hells,
In being deprived of everlasting bliss?   80
O Faustus, leave these frivolous demands,
Which strike a terror to my fainting soul.

FAUSTUS

What, is great Mephostophilis so passionate
For being deprived of the joys of heaven?
Learn thou of Faustus manly fortitude,   85
And scorn those joys thou never shalt possess.
Go bear these tidings to great Lucifer,
Seeing Faustus hath incurred eternal death,
By desperate thoughts against Jove's deity:
Say he surrenders up to him his soul,   90
So he will spare him four and twenty years,
Letting him live in all voluptuousness,
Having thee ever to attend on me,
To give me whatsoever I shall ask;
To tell me whatsoever I demand: 95
To slay mine enemies, and aid my friends,
And always be obedient to my will.
Go, and return to mighty Lucifer,
And meet me in my study, at midnight,
And then resolve me of thy master's mind.   100

MEPHOSTOPHILIS

I will Faustus.   *Exit*

91 *So* On condition that

76–80 Caxton, while locating hell 'in the most lowest place, moste derke,
and most vyle of the erthe', stressed that it is a state as well as a place;
the sinner is like a man 'that had a grete maladye, so moche that he
shold deye, and that he were brought in to a fair place and plesaunt
for to have Joye and solace; of so moche shold he be more hevy and
sorowful' (*The Mirrour of the World* (1480), ii, 18). Marlowe's concept
of hell at this point may be compared with Milton's; like Mephostophilis,
Satan cannot escape.

> for within him Hell
> He brings, and round about him, nor from Hell
> One step, no more than from himself can fly
> By change of place.
>   *Paradise Lost*, iv, 20–23.

Mephostophilis' account of the torment of deprivation is translated
from St. John Chrysostom: '*si decem mille gehennas quis dixerit, nihil
tale est quale ab illa beata visione excidere*' (see John Searle, *T.L.S.*, 15th
February 1936).

FAUSTUS
Had I as many souls as there be stars
I'd give them all for Mephostophilis.
By him, I'll be great emperor of the world,
And make a bridge through the moving air   105
To pass the ocean with a band of men;
I'll join the hills that bind the Afric shore,
And make that country continent to Spain,
And both contributory to my crown.
The emperor shall not live, but by my leave,   110
Nor any potentate of Germany.
Now that I have obtained what I desired
I'll live in speculation of this art
Till Mephostophilis return again.   *Exit*

Act I, Scene iv

Enter WAGNER *and the* CLOWN

WAGNER
Come hither sirra boy.

107 *hills . . . shore* The hills on either side of the straits of Gibraltar
    which, if joined, would unite Africa and Europe into a single
    continent

Act I, Scene iv. It is not easy to account for all the variants between A and
B in this scene. A's *pickadevants* (1.3) is supported against B's *beards*
by the imitation of this in the anonymous *Taming of A Shrew.* The
'French crowns' passage (11.26–9) has hitherto been rejected on
historical grounds (but see note below) and Greg discards the 'kill-
devil' lines (35–9) with the argument that these are borrowed from
Looking Glass for London (see Introduction p. xvii). Two passages in
the A Text were almost certainly interpolated by the comedians. When
the devils have vanished the Clown comments:

> What, are they gone? A vengeance on them, they have vile long
> nails; there was a he-devil and a she-devil; I'll tell you how you
> shall know them: all he-devils has horns, and all she-devils has
> clifts and cloven feet.

At Wagner's promise of the power of metamorphosis the Clown is at
first disapproving and then lewdly appreciative:

> How? A Christian fellow to a dog, or a cat, a mouse or a rat? No,
> no, sir, if you turn me into anything, let it be in the likeness of a
> little pretty frisking flea, that I may be here and there and every-
> where. O I'll tickle the pretty wenches' plackets, I'll be amongst
> them i'faith.

CLOWN

Boy? O disgrace to my person! Zounds, boy in your face!
You have seen many boys with such pickadevants, I am sure.

WAGNER

Sirra, hast thou no comings in?

CLOWN

Yes, and goings out too, you may see sir.   5

WAGNER

Alas poor slave, see how poverty jests in his nakedness. The
villain is bare and out of service, and so hungry, that I know
he would give his soul to the devil, for a shoulder of mutton,
though it were blood-raw.

CLOWN

Not so neither! I had need to have it well roasted, and good   10
sauce to it, if I pay so dear, I can tell you.

WAGNER

Sirra, wilt thou be my man and wait on me? And I will
make thee go, like *Qui mihi discipulus*.

CLOWN

What, in verse?

WAGNER

No slave, in beaten silk, and stavesacre,   15

CLOWN

Stavesacre? That's good to kill vermin; then, belike, if I
serve you, I shall be lousy.

WAGNER

Why, so thou shalt be, whether thou dost it or no: for sirra,

3 *pickadevants* A (beards B) beards fashionably cut to a small
    point (French *pic à devant*)
4 *comings in* earnings, income
5 *goings out* expenses; but the Clown makes the word serve two
    functions, pointing also to his tattered clothing
7 *out of service* out of a job
13 *Qui mihi discipulus* You who are my pupil; the opening words of
    a didactic Latin poem by the schoolmaster William Lily which
    would be familiar to every grammar school boy

---

15 *beaten silk, and stavesacre* 'In effect Wagner promises to dress his servant
    (or rather to dress him down) in silk—and adds that plenty of Keating's
    powder will be needed' (Greg). Gold or silver was hammered into silk
    as a kind of embroidery; *stavesacre* was a preparation from delphinium
    seeds used for killing fleas. It has been suggested that the Clown's
    stavesacre is a comic corruption of what Wagner actually said. But the
    A Clown interpolates here 'Knavesacre? Ay, I thought that was all the
    land his father left him: do you hear, I would be sorry to rob you of your
    living'. Whether this has any authority or not, it shows that Wagner's
    word must have been *stavesacre;* a script writer would not use the same
    kind of joke twice.

if thou dost not presently bind thyself to me for seven years,
I'll turn all the lice about thee into familiars, and make them   20
tear thee in pieces.

CLOWN

Nay sir, you may save yourself a labour, for they are as
familiar with me, as if they paid for their meat and drink, I
can tell you.

WAGNER

Well sirra, leave your jesting, and take these guilders.   25

CLOWN

Gridirons, what be they?

WAGNER

Why, French crowns.

CLOWN

Mass, but for the name of French crowns a man were as
good have as many English counters.

WAGNER

So, now thou art to be at an hour's warning, whensoever,   30
and wheresoever the devil shall fetch thee.

CLOWN

Here, take your guilders again, I'll none of 'em.

WAGNER

Not I, thou art pressed, prepare thyself, for I will presently
raise up two devils to carry thee away: Baliol and Belcher!

CLOWN

Let your Balio and your Belcher come here, and I'll knock   35

20 *familiars* familiar spirits, diabolic personal attendants
23 they treat me as contemptuously as if they were customers at an
   inn who pay for what they consume
29 *counters* worthless tokens
33 *pressed* enlisted; the taking of money was a token of enrolment for
   military service
34 *Baliol* A (Banio B) probably a corruption of Belial
35 *knock* thump, beat

26–9 French crowns, legal tender in England in the 16th and early 17th
   centuries, were easily counterfeited. Marlowe himself is reported in the
   Baines' Libel as having boasted 'That he had as good Right to Coine as
   the Queen of England and that . . . he ment, through the help of a
   Cunninge stamp maker to Coin ffrench Crownes pistoletes and English
   shillinges'. Among government measures to stop the flood of false coins
   was a proclamation of 1587 urging all who were offered such pieces to
   strike a hole in them (See Ruding, *Annals of the Coinage of Britain*,
   (1817), i, 192 ff); perhaps the Clown refers to the holes in the coins when
   he describes them as *gridirons*. (See H. E. Cain, 'Marlowe's "French
   Crowns" ', *M.L.N.*, XLIX (1934), 380–84.) The money market
   under James was less troubled by this kind of counterfeiting, and the
   passage may have been omitted from B because it was no longer meaning-
   ful.

them, they were never so knocked since they were devils.
Say I should kill one of them, what would folks say? 'Do ye
see yonder tall fellow in the round slop, he has killed the
devil!' So I should be called kill-devil all the parish over.

Enter two DEVILS *and the* CLOWN
runs up and down crying

WAGNER

How now sir, will you serve me now?   40
CLOWN

Ay good Wagner, take away the devil then.
WAGNER

Spirits away!   *Exeunt* [DEVILS]
     Now sirra, follow me.
CLOWN

I will sir; but hark you master, will you teach me this
conjuring occupation?
WAGNER

Ay sirra, I'll teach thee to turn thyself to a dog, or a cat, or   45
a mouse, or a rat, or anything.
CLOWN

A dog, or a cat, or a mouse, or a rat? O brave, Wagner.
WAGNER

Villain, call me Master Wagner, and see that you walk
attentively, and let your right eye be always diametrally
fixed upon my left heel, that thou may'st *quasi vestigias*   50
nostras insistere.
CLOWN

Well sir, I warrant you.   *Exeunt*

Act II, Scene i

Enter FAUSTUS *in his study*

FAUSTUS

Now Faustus must thou needs be damned
And canst thou not be saved?
What boots it then to think on God or heaven?

38 *tall* brave;
   round slop baggy trousers
49 *diametrally* diametrically
50–51 *quasi vestigias nostras insistere* as it were tread in our footsteps;
   the construction is false (for *vestigiis nostris*) but this may be
   intentional

Away with such vain fancies and despair,
Despair in God, and trust in Belzebub.   5
Now go not backward: no, Faustus, be resolute,
Why waverest thou? O, something soundeth in mine ears:
'Abjure this magic, turn to God again'.
Ay, and Faustus will turn to God again.
To God? He loves thee not: 10
The God thou servest is thine own appetite
Wherein is fixed the love of Belzebub:
To him, I'll build an altar and a church,
And offer luke-warm blood of new-born babes.

Enter the two ANGELS

GOOD ANGEL
Sweet Faustus, leave that execrable art.   15
FAUSTUS
Contrition, prayer, repentance – what of these?
GOOD ANGEL
O they are means to bring thee unto heaven.
BAD ANGEL
Rather illusions, fruits of lunacy,
That make men foolish that do trust them most.
GOOD ANGEL
Sweet Faustus, think of heaven, and heavenly things.   20
BAD ANGEL
No Faustus, think of honour and of wealth.

Exeunt ANGELS

FAUSTUS
Wealth!
Why, the signory of Emden shall be mine:
When Mephostophilis shall stand by me
What god can hurt me? Faustus thou art safe.   25
Cast no more doubts; Mephostophilis, come
And bring glad tidings from great Lucifer.

9–10 *Ay . . . God* A (*not in* B)
23 *signory of Emden* governorship of Emden – a port on the mouth of
the Ems, at this time trading extensively with England
25 *god* A (power B)

15 Before this line B inserts:
   Evil Angel Go forward Faustus, in that famous art.
   The line exactly repeats I.i, 73, and this alone makes it suspect. Furthermore, the inconsistency of the speech heading (*Evil* instead of *Bad*) points
   to some kind of tinkering with the text. The same inconsistency is to be
   found at II.ii, 17, but here B has borrowed the line and its heading from A.

Is't not midnight? Come Mephostophilis,
Veni, veni Mephostophilis.

Enter MEPHOSTOPHILIS

Now tell me what saith Lucifer thy lord?   30
MEPHOSTOPHILIS
That I shall wait on Faustus whilst he lives,
So he will buy my service with his soul.
FAUSTUS
Already Faustus hath hazarded that for thee.
MEPHOSTOPHILIS
But now thou must bequeath it solemnly,
And write a deed of gift with thine own blood;   35
For that security craves Lucifer.
If thou deny it I must back to hell.
FAUSTUS
Stay Mephostophilis, and tell me,
What good will my soul do thy lord?
MEPHOSTOPHILIS
Enlarge his kingdom.   40
FAUSTUS
Is that the reason why he tempts us thus?
MEPHOSTOPHILIS
Solamen miseris, socios habuisse doloris.
FAUSTUS
Why, have you any pain that torture others?
MEPHOSTOPHILIS
As great as have the human souls of men.
But tell me Faustus, shall I have thy soul?   45
And I will be thy slave and wait on thee,
And give thee more than thou hast wit to ask.
FAUSTUS
Ay Mephostophilis, I'll give it him.
MEPHOSTOPHILIS
Then Faustus, stab thine arm courageously,
And bind thy soul, that at some certain day   50

29 Come, O come Mephostophilis
33 *hazarded* jeopardized
42 In Chaucer's version: 'Men seyn, "to wrecche is consolacioun
    To have an-other felawe in his peyne".' *Troilus and Criseyde,* i,
    708-9.

40 'Satan's chiefest drift & main point that he aimeth at, is the inlargement
    of his owne kingdom, by the eternall destruction of man in the life to
    come', James Mason, *The Anatomie of Sorcerie* (1612), p. 55.

Great Lucifer may claim it as his own,
And then be thou as great as Lucifer.

FAUSTUS

Lo Mephostophilis, for love of thee
                    [*stabs his arm*]
Faustus hath cut his arm, and with his proper blood
Assures his soul to be great Lucifer's,   55
Chief lord and regent of perpetual night.
View here this blood that trickles from mine arm,
And let it be propitious for my wish.

MEPHOSTOPHILIS

But Faustus,
Write it in manner of a deed of gift.   60

FAUSTUS

Ay, so I will.
                    [*writes*]
          But Mephostophilis,
My blood congeals, and I can write no more.

MEPHOSTOPHILIS

I'll fetch thee fire to dissolve it straight.

                                        Exit

FAUSTUS

What might the staying of my blood portend?
Is it unwilling I should write this bill?   65
Why streams it not, that I may write afresh?
'Faustus gives to thee his soul': ah, there it stayed!
Why should'st thou not? Is not thy soul thine own?
Then write again: 'Faustus gives to thee his soul'.

          Enter MEPHOSTOPHILIS *with the*
                    Chafer of Fire

MEPHOSTOPHILIS

See Faustus here is fire, set it on.   70

FAUSTUS

So, now the blood begins to clear again:
                              [*writes again*]
Now will I make an end immediately.

MEPHOSTOPHILIS

What will not I do to obtain his soul!

54 *proper* own
69 s.d. *Chafer* portable grate
70 *set it on* 'set his blood in a saucer on warm ashes'. *EFB*,vi.
71 Greg observes that no earthly fire will liquefy congealed blood

FAUSTUS

Consummatum est: this bill is ended,
And Faustus hath bequeathed his soul to Lucifer   75
But what is this inscription on mine arm?
Homo fuge! Whither should I fly?
If unto God, he'll throw me down to hell.
My senses are deceived, here's nothing writ:
O yes, I see it plain, even here is writ   80
Homo fuge! Yet shall not Faustus fly.

MEPHOSTOPHILIS

I'll fetch him somewhat to delight his mind.

                                                                 Exit

        Enter DEVILS, *giving crowns and rich apparel*
        to FAUSTUS: *they dance, and then depart:*
              Enter MEPHOSTOPHILIS

FAUSTUS

What means this show? Speak Mephostophilis.

MEPHOSTOPHILIS

Nothing Faustus, but to delight thy mind,
And let thee see what magic can perform.   85

FAUSTUS

But may I raise such spirits when I please?

MEPHOSTOPHILIS

Ay Faustus, and do greater things than these.

FAUSTUS

Then Mephostophilis, receive this scroll.
A deed of gift, of body and of soul:
But yet conditionally, that thou perform   90
All covenants and articles between us both.

MEPHOSTOPHILIS

Faustus, I swear by hell and Lucifer,
To effect all promises between us made.

FAUSTUS

Then hear me read it Mephostophilis.
On these conditions following: 95
   First, that Faustus may be a spirit in form and substance.

74 *Consummatum est* It is finished; the last words of Christ on the
   cross: St. John, xix,30
77 *Homo fuge* Fly, O man   78 *God* A (heaven B)
88 A gives Faustus another line before this one: 'Then there's
   enough for a thousand souls.'

96 *spirit* A spirit, to the Elizabethans, was usually an evil one, a devil (see
   Shakespeare, Sonnet CXLIV); according to some theologians, who
   followed Aquinas, God could have no mercy on a devil who was *ipso
   facto* incapable of repenting. See II.ii, 13–15.

Secondly, that Mephostophilis shall be his servant, and at
his command.
Thirdly, that Mephostophilis shall do for him, and bring
him whatsoever.   100
Fourthly, that he shall be in his chamber or house invisible.
Lastly, that he shall appear to the said John Faustus, at all
times, in what form or shape soever he please.
I, John Faustus of Wittenberg. doctor, by these presents, do
give both body and soul to Lucifer, Prince of the East, and   105
his minister Mephostophilis, and furthermore grant unto
them, that four and twenty years being expired, the articles
above written inviolate, full power to fetch or carry the said
John Faustus, body and soul, flesh, blood, or goods, into
their habitation wheresoever.   110

By me John Faustus

MEPHOSTOPHILIS

Speak Faustus, do you deliver this as your deed?

FAUSTUS

Ay, take it, and the devil give thee good on't.

MEPHOSTOPHILIS

Now Faustus, ask what thou wilt.

FAUSTUS

First will I question with thee about hell: 115
Tell me, where is the place that men call hell?

MEPHOSTOPHILIS

Under the heavens.

FAUSTUS

Ay, so are all things else; but whereabouts?

MEPHOSTOPHILIS

Within the bowels of these elements,
Where we are tortured, and remain for ever.   120
Hell hath no limits, nor is circumscribed
In one self place; but where we are is hell,
And where hell is, there must we ever be.
And to be short, when all the world dissolves,
And every creature shall be purified,   125
All places shall be hell that is not heaven.

FAUSTUS

I think hell's a fable.

MEPHOSTOPHILIS

Ay, think so still, till experience change thy mind.

---

104 *these presents* the legal articles
119 *these elements* the four elements below the sphere of the moon
122 *one self place* one particular place

FAUSTUS

Why, dost thou think that Faustus shall be damned?

MEPHOSTOPHILIS

Ay, of necessity, for here's the scroll   130
In which thou hast given thy soul to Lucifer.

FAUSTUS

Ay, and body too, but what of that?
Think'st thou that Faustus is so fond to imagine,
That after this life there is any pain?
No, these are trifles, and mere old wives' tales.   135

MEPHOSTOPHILIS

But I am an instance to prove the contrary:
For I tell thee I am damned, and now in hell.

FAUSTUS

Nay, and this be hell, I'll willingly be damned.
What, sleeping, eating, walking and disputing?
But leaving this, let me have a wife, the fairest maid in   140
Germany, for I am wanton and lascivious, and cannot live
without a wife.

MEPHOSTOPHILIS

How, a wife? I prithee Faustus, talk not of a wife.

FAUSTUS

Nay sweet Mephostophilis, fetch me one, for I will have one.

MEPHOSTOPHILIS

Well, thou wilt have one; sit there till I come;   145
I'll fetch thee a wife in the devil's name.   [*Exit*]

Enter with a DEVIL *dressed like a woman, with fireworks*

MEPHOSTOPHILIS

Tell me Faustus, how dost thou like thy wife?

FAUSTUS

A plague on her for a hot whore! No, I'll no wife.

MEPHOSTOPHILIS

Marriage is but a ceremonial toy,
And if thou lovest me think no more of it.   150
I'll cull thee out the fairest courtesans,
And bring them every morning to thy bed:
She whom thine eye shall like, thy heart shall have,
Were she as chaste as was Penelope,

133 *fond foolish*
151 *cull* pick
154 *Penelope* wife of Ulysses, renowned for her fidelity to a lost husband

139–47 A gives the fuller text here; the abrupt change to prose, in both
versions, suggests that another author has taken over.

As wise as Saba, or as beautiful   155
As was bright Lucifer before his fall.
Hold, take this book, peruse it thoroughly:
The iterating of these lines brings gold;
The framing of this circle on the ground
Brings thunder, whirlwinds, storm and lightning: 160
Pronounce this thrice devoutly to thyself,
And men in harness shall appear to thee,
Ready to execute what thou command'st.

FAUSTUS

Thanks Mephostophilis; yet fain would I have a book
wherein I might behold all spells and incantations, that I   165
might raise up spirits when I please.

MEPHOSTOPHILIS

Here they are in this book.   *There turn to them*

FAUSTUS

Now would I have a book where I might see all characters
and planets of the heavens, that I might know their motions
and dispositions.   170

MEPHOSTOPHILIS

Here they are too.   *Turn to them*

FAUSTUS

Nay, let me have one book more, and then I have done,
wherein I might see all plants, herbs and trees that grow
upon the earth.

MEPHOSTOPHILIS

Here they be.   175

FAUSTUS

O thou art deceived.

MEPHOSTOPHILIS

Tut I warrant thee.   *Turn to them*
                                              Exeunt

---

155 *Saba* the Queen of Sheba, who confronted Solomon with 'hard
    questions', I Kings, x
162 *harness* armour
170 *dispositions* situations

163–76 B allows no investigation of the magic book, ending the episode
    abruptly with Faustus' thanks:

    Thanks Mephostophilis for this sweet book.
    This will I keep as chary as my life.

    Although the sudden switch in A from verse to prose suggests another
    author, or even an after-thought, B's anticipation of II.ii, 172 is equally
    suspicious.

Act II, Scene ii

Enter FAUSTUS *in his study*
and MEPHOSTOPHILIS

FAUSTUS

When I behold the heavens then I repent
And curse thee wicked Mephostophilis,
Because thou hast deprived me of those joys.

MEPHOSTOPHILIS

'Twas thine own seeking Faustus, thank thyself:
But think'st thou heaven is such a glorious thing?   5
I tell thee Faustus, it is not half so fair
As thou, or any man that breathes on earth.

FAUSTUS

How prov'st thou that?

MEPHOSTOPHILIS

'Twas made for man; then he's more excellent.

FAUSTUS

If heaven was made for man, 'twas made for me: 10
I will renounce this magic and repent.

Enter the two ANGELS

GOOD ANGEL

Faustus repent, yet God will pity thee.

BAD ANGEL

Thou art a spirit, God cannot pity thee.

FAUSTUS

Who buzzeth in mine ears I am a spirit?
Be I a devil yet God may pity me,   15
Yea, God will pity me if I repent.

4 B (*not in* A)
13 (see note on II.i, 96)
14 *buzzeth* whispers
15 *Be I* This could mean either 'Even if I am' or else 'Even though
I were'

Act II, Scene ii. Both texts seem to have lost a scene here; the Elizabethans
would never take two characters off the stage to bring them on again
immediately. Boas suggests a comic interlude with Wagner, Greg an
episode in preparation for II.iii, showing the Clown stealing one of
Faustus' conjuring books and determining to leave Wagner's service.
But the Clown of I.iv seems to me to be a different kind of comedian
from the Robin of the subsequent comic scenes (see Introduction
p. xvi).

EVIL ANGEL

Ay, but Faustus never shall repent. *Exeunt* ANGELS

FAUSTUS

My heart's so hardened I cannot repent!
Scarce can I name salvation, faith, or heaven,
But fearful echoes thunders in mine ears, 20
'Faustus, thou art damned': then swords and knives,
Poison, guns, halters and envenomed steel
Are laid before me to dispatch myself:
And long ere this, I should have done the deed,
Had not sweet pleasure conquered deep despair. 25
Have not I made blind Homer sing to me
Of Alexander's love, and Oenon's death?
And hath not he, that built the walls of Thebes
With ravishing sound of his melodious harp,
Made music with my Mephostophilis? 30
Why should I die then, or basely despair?
I am resolved! Faustus shall not repent.
Come Mephostophilis let us dispute again,
And reason of divine astrology.
Speak, are there many spheres above the moon? 35
Are all celestial bodies but one globe,
As is the substance of this centric earth?

MEPHOSTOPHILIS

As are the elements, such are the heavens,
Even from the moon unto the empyreal orb,
Mutually folded in each other's spheres, 40

17 (see note on II.i, 15)
22 *halters* hangman's ropes
24 *done the deed* B (slain myself A)
39 B (*not in* A)

---

27 *Alexander . . . death* Alexander, Homer's name for Paris son of Priam,
fell in love with Oenone before he encountered Helen; wounded in the
Trojan War, he was carried to Oenone and died at her feet, whereupon
she stabbed herself.
28–9 At the sound of Amphion's harp the stones were so affected that
they rose of their own accord to form the walls of Thebes.
35–62 The Faustus of Marlowe's source was an astrologer–a calendar-
maker and weather-forecaster–rather than an astronomer, and although
Mephostophilis promises to teach him about the planets the approach
is unscientific and the information a miscellaneous jumble. Marlowe's
protagonist has the questioning mind of the Renaissance student, and
the answers he is given accord with the sceptical authorities of the day
(See Kocher, pp. 214–23, and F. R. Johnson, 'Marlowe's Astronomy
and Renaissance Skepticism', *E.L.H.*, XIII (1946), iv). The Ptolemaic

And jointly move upon one axletree,
Whose termine is termed the world's wide pole.
Nor are the names of Saturn, Mars or Jupiter,
Feigned, but are erring stars.

FAUSTUS

But have they all one motion, both *situ et tempore*?   45

MEPHOSTOPHILIS

All move from east to west in four and twenty hours, upon
the poles of the world, but differ in their motions upon the
poles of the zodiac.

FAUSTUS

These slender questions Wagner can decide!
Hath Mephostophilis no greater skill?   50
Who knows not the double motion of the planets?
That the first is finished in a natural day, the second thus:

42 *termine* boundary (astronomical)
45 *situ et tempore* in direction and in time
49 *questions* B (trifles A)

---

system, as yet unshaken by Copernicus, held that the universe was
composed of concentric spheres with the earth (*this centric earth*) as
the innermost. Beyond the earth was the sphere of the Moon, and
further out still the spheres of the six other *erring stars* or planets:
Mercury, Venus, Sun, Mars, Jupiter, Saturn. The eighth was the
firmament, or sphere of the fixed stars, which Marlowe, admitting only
nine spheres (1.59) identified with the *Primum Mobile*, the first moving
thing which imparted movement to all the rest. The ninth sphere
(tenth, if the *Primum Mobile* was allowed to be separate from the
firmament) was the immoveable empyrean (*the empyreal orb*).

35–44 Faustus asks first for confirmation of the number of spheres beyond
the Moon and whether in fact these do form a single ball. Mephostophilis replies that just as the four elements enclose each other (earth is
surrounded by water, water by air, and air by fire), so each sphere or
heaven is circled round by the ones beyond it, and all rotate upon a
single axletree. Saturn, Mars and the other planets are individually
recognizable and are called *erring* or wandering stars to distinguish
them from the fixed stars joined to the firmament.

45–56 'Do all the planets move at the same speed and in the same direction?'
is Faustus' next question. He is told that the planets have two movements: a daily east to west rotation round the earth governed by the
Primum Mobile, and a slower, individual turning from west to east.
Caxton (*Mirrour of the World*, (1480), i.13) explains that each planet is
like a fly crawling on a wheel; if the fly crawls in one direction and the
wheel turns in the opposite, the fly may be said to have two movements.
Faustus knows this well enough, and proceeds to detail with reasonable
accuracy the different times taken by the planets in their individual
revolutions–the farthest from the earth, naturally, taking the longest.
The figures usually given are: Saturn $29\frac{1}{2}$ years; Jupiter $11\frac{3}{4}$ years;
Mars 1 year 11 months; Sun 1 year; Venus $7\frac{1}{2}$ months; and Mercury
3 months.

Saturn in thirty years; Jupiter in twelve; Mars in four; the
Sun, Venus and Mercury in a year; the Moon in twenty-
eight days. These are freshmen's suppositions. But tell me,   55
hath every sphere a dominion or intelligentia?

MEPHOSTOPHILIS

Ay.

FAUSTUS

How many heavens, or spheres, are there?

MEPHOSTOPHILIS

Nine: the seven planets, the firmament, and the empyreal
heaven.   60

FAUSTUS

But is there not *coelum igneum? et cristallinum?*

MEPHOSTOPHILIS

No Faustus, they be but fables.

FAUSTUS

Resolve me then in this one question: why are not conjunctions, oppositions, aspects, eclipses, all at one time,
but in some years we have more, in some less?   65

MEPHOSTOPHILIS

Per inaequalem motum, respectu totius.

FAUSTUS

Well, I am answered. Now tell me who made the world?

MEPHOSTOPHILIS

I will not.

FAUSTUS

Sweet Mephostophilis, tell me.

55 *suppositions* A (questions B) elementary facts given to first year
   undergraduates for them to build an argument on

56–7 The next question at issue relates to a theory first propounded by
   Plato and developed in the Middle Ages, that each planet was guided
   by an angelic spirit, commonly called the *intelligence*:

> Let mans Soule be a Spheare, and then, in this,
> The intelligence that moves, devotion is,
>> Donne, 'Good Friday, Riding Westwards'

   Mephostophilis affirms the *intelligence*, but the theory was never really
   accepted by scientists.

58–62 Faustus seems to return to his earlier query about the number of
   spheres or heavens. Aristotle accounted for eight, but another was
   added by the early Church Fathers who postulated the *empyreal heaven*
   which was the abode of God, unmoving and shining with a piercing,
   stainless light. Mephostophilis contradicts the current belief that there
   were still more celestial spheres, the *coelum igneum* and *coelum cristallinum* (heavens of fire and crystal). Both these were added to the
   Aristotelian concept of the universe (the latter by Ptolemy) and Marlowe
   was not alone in denying their existence. Pierre de La Primaudaye,
   whose *French Academie* (vol. III) is a possible source for Marlowe's
   astronomical knowledge, shares this doubt.

MEPHOSTOPHILIS

Move me not Faustus.   70

FAUSTUS

Villain, have not I bound thee to tell me anything?

MEPHOSTOPHILIS

Ay, that is not against our kingdom.

This is: thou art damned, think thou on hell.

FAUSTUS

Think, Faustus, upon God, that made the world.

MEPHOSTOPHILIS

Remember this!   75

Exit

FAUSTUS

Ay, go accursed spirit to ugly hell:

'Tis thou hast damned distressed Faustus' soul.

Is't not too late?

Enter the two ANGELS

BAD ANGEL

Too late.

GOOD ANGEL

Never too late, if Faustus will repent.   80

BAD ANGEL

If thou repent, devils will tear thee in pieces.

GOOD ANGEL

Repent, and they shall never raze thy skin.

Exeunt ANGELS

70 *Move* Vex
82 *raze* graze

63–6 Mephostophilis' answer to the next question sounds like a quotation
   from some astronomical textbook. Faustus asks about the behaviour
   of the planets, using technical but well-known astronomical terms:
   conjunctions are the apparent joinings together of two planets, while
   oppositions describes their relationships when most remote:

>   Therefore the love which us doth bind,
>   But Fate so enviously debarrs,
>   Is the Conjunction of the Mind,
>   And Opposition of the Stars.
>   Marvell, 'The Definition of Love'.

Any position between the two extremes of conjunction and opposition
was termed an *aspect*. To astrologers the differing situations and
relations of the planets all have some particular significance–hence the
horoscope. Faustus is finally told what he already knows: that the
heavenly bodies do not all move at the same speed, and that for this
reason ('through an irregular motion so far as the whole is concerned',
1.66) there are more eclipses etc. in some years than in others.

FAUSTUS

O Christ my saviour, my saviour,
Help to save distressed Faustus' soul.

Enter LUCIFER, BELZEBUB, *and* MEPHOSTOPHILIS

LUCIFER

Christ cannot save thy soul, for he is just;   85
There's none but I have interest in the same.

FAUSTUS

O what art thou that look'st so terribly?

LUCIFER

I am Lucifer, and this is my companion prince in hell.

FAUSTUS

O Faustus, they are come to fetch thy soul!

BELZEBUB

We are come to tell thee thou dost injure us.   90

LUCIFER

Thou call'st on Christ contrary to thy promise.

BELZEBUB

Thou should'st not think on God.

LUCIFER

Think on the devil.

BELZEBUB

And his dam too.

FAUSTUS

Nor will I henceforth: pardon me in this,   95
And Faustus vows never to look to heaven,
Never to name God, or to pray to him,
To burn his scriptures, slay his ministers,
And make my spirits pull his churches down.

LUCIFER

So shalt thou show thyself an obedient servant,   100
And we will highly gratify thee for it.

BELZEBUB

Faustus, we are come from hell in person to show thee some
pastime: sit down and thou shalt behold the Seven Deadly
Sins appear to thee in their own proper shapes and likeness.

FAUSTUS

That sight will be as pleasing unto me as Paradise was to   105
Adam the first day of his creation.

84 *Help* B (Seek A)
86 *interest in* legal claim on
97–9 A (*not in* B)

LUCIFER

Talk not of Paradise or creation, but mark the show.
Go Mephostophilis, fetch them in.

Enter the SEVEN DEADLY SINS

BELZEBUB

Now Faustus, examine them of their several names and
dispositions.   110

FAUSTUS

That shall I soon: what art thou, the first?

PRIDE

I am Pride; I disdain to have any parents: I am like to
Ovid's flea, I can creep into every corner of a wench: sometimes, like a periwig, I sit upon her brow; next, like a neck-
lace, I hang about her neck; then, like a fan of feathers, I   115
kiss her lips; and then, turning myself to a wrought smock,
do what I list. But fie, what a smell is here! I'll not speak
another word unless the ground be perfumed, and covered
with cloth of arras.

FAUSTUS

Thou art a proud knave indeed: what art thou, the second?   120

COVETOUSNESS

I am Covetousness, begotten of an old churl in a leather
bag; and might I now obtain my wish, this house, you and
all should turn to gold, that I might lock you safe into my
chest. O my sweet gold!

FAUSTUS

And what art thou, the third?   125

ENVY

I am Envy, begotten of a chimney-sweeper, and an oyster-
wife: I cannot read, and therefore wish all books burnt. I
am lean with seeing others eat: O that there would come a
famine over all the world, that all might die, and I live
alone, then thou shouldst see how fat I'd be. But must thou   130
sit, and I stand? Come down, with a vengeance.

113 *Ovid's flea* The poet of 'The Song of the Flea' (probably medieval
   but attributed to Ovid) envies the flea for its freedom of movement
   over his mistress' body
116 *wrought* embroidered
117 *another word* A (a word more for a king's ransom B); B anticipates
   the words of Sloth (below, 157–8)
119 *cloth of arras* tapestry; woven at Arras in Flanders and used for
   wall-hangings
121 *leather bag* the miser's purse
126–7 *begotten . . . wife* 'and therefore black and malodorous' (Wheeler)

R—C

FAUSTUS

Out, envious wretch! But what art thou, the fourth?

WRATH

I am Wrath: I had neither father nor mother; I leapt out
of a lion's mouth when I was scarce an hour old, and ever
since have run up and down the world with these case of   135
rapiers, wounding myself when I could get none to fight
withal: I was born in hell, and look to it, for some of you
shall be my father.

FAUSTUS

And what art thou, the fifth?

GLUTTONY

I am gluttony; my parents are all dead, and the devil a   140
penny they have left me, but a small pension, and that buys
me thirty meals a day, and ten bevers: a small trifle to
suffice nature. I come of a royal pedigree: my father was a
gammon of bacon, and my mother was a hogshead of claret
wine. My godfathers were these: Peter Pickled-Herring and   145
Martin Martlemass-Beef: O but my godmother, she was a
jolly gentlewoman, and well beloved in every good town and
city; her name was Mistress Margery March-Beer. Now
Faustus, thou hast heard all my progeny, wilt thou bid me
to supper?   150

FAUSTUS

No, I'll see thee hanged, thou wilt eat up all my victuals.

GLUTTONY

Then the devil choke thee.

FAUSTUS

Choke thyself, Glutton; what art thou, the sixth?

SLOTH

Hey ho! I am Sloth: I was begotten on a sunny bank, where
I have lain ever since, and you have done me great injury   155
to bring me from thence; let me be carried thither again by
Gluttony and Lechery. Hey ho, I'll not speak a word more
for a king's ransom.

135 *these case* A case of rapiers is in fact a pair
142 *bevers* snacks
146 *Martlemass-Beef* Meat, salted to preserve it for winter, was hung
up to Martinmas (November 11th)
147–8 *a jolly ... city* A (an ancient gentlewoman B)
148 *March-Beer* a rich ale, made in March and left to mature for at
least two years
149 *progeny* lineage (obsolete)
154–7 *where ... Lechery* A (*not in* B)

FAUSTUS

And what are you Mistress Minx, the seventh and last?

LECHERY

Who I? I sir? I am one that loves an inch of raw mutton,   160
better than an ell of fried stockfish: and the first letter of
my name begins with Lechery.

LUCIFER

Away to hell, away, on piper.   *Exeunt the* SEVEN SINS

FAUSTUS

O how this sight doth delight my soul.

LUCIFER

But Faustus, in hell is all manner of delight.   165

FAUSTUS

O might I see hell, and return again safe, how happy were
I then.

LUCIFER

Faustus, thou shalt, at midnight I will send for thee;
Meanwhile peruse this book, and view it throughly,
And thou shalt turn thyself into what shape thou wilt.   170

FAUSTUS

Thanks mighty Lucifer:
This will I keep as chary as my life.

LUCIFER

Now Faustus, farewell.

FAUSTUS

Farewell, great Lucifer: come Mephostophilis.
                    Exeunt omnes, several ways

---

162 *begins with Lechery* A common form of jest: 'Her name begins
    with Mistress Purge', Middleton, *The Family of Love*, II.iii, 53
169 *throughly* thoroughly
172 *chary* carefully
174 s.d. *several ways* in different directions

160–1 *loves . . . stockfish* Most editors are reticent about the meaning of this
    line and content themselves with pointing out that *mutton* is frequently
    used to mean 'prostitute'. Greg observes that such an interpretation
    cannot apply where Lechery is *Mistress Minx*, and he adds 'but this
    indelicate subject need not be pursued. Ward by omitting the passage
    showed that he understood it'. Lechery is saying in effect that she prefers
    a small quantity of virility to a large extent of impotence. *Stock-fish*, a
    long dried-up piece of cod, is a common term of abuse, indicating
    impotence: 'he was begot between two stockfishes', *Measure for
    Measure*, III.ii, 98.

Act II, Scene iii

Enter the CLOWN [ROBIN]

CLOWN
What, Dick, look to the horses there till I come again. I have
gotten one of Doctor Faustus' conjuring books, and now
we'll have such knavery, as't passes.

Enter DICK

DICK
What, Robin, you must come away and walk the horses.
ROBIN
I walk the horses! I scorn't, 'faith, I have other matters in   5
hand, let the horses walk themselves and they will. [*reads*]
'A *per se* a; t. h. e. the; o *per se* o; deny orgon, gorgon'. Keep
further from me, O thou illiterate and unlearned ostler.
DICK
'Snails, what hast thou got there? A book? Why, thou canst
not tell ne'er a word on't.   10
ROBIN
That thou shalt see presently: keep out of the circle, I say,
lest I send you into the hostry with a vengeance.
DICK
That's like, 'faith: you had best leave your foolery, for an
my master come, he'll conjure you, 'faith.
ROBIN
My master conjure me? I'll tell thee what, an my master   15
come here, I'll clap as fair a pair of horns on's head as e'er
thou sawest in thy life.
DICK
Thou needest not do that, for my mistress hath done it.
ROBIN
Ay, there be of us here, that have waded as deep into matters,
as other men, if they were disposed to talk.   20

II.iii. A's version of this scene is printed in the Appendix (p. 90)
   3 *as't passes* as beats everything
   7 *per se* by itself; a by itself spells a
     deny orgon, gorgon Robin is struggling to read the 'Demogorgon'
     of Faustus' invocation
   9 *'Snails* By God's nails
  12 *hostry* hostelry, inn
  13 *That's like* A likely chance
  19 *matters* affairs; 'I meddle with no tradesman's matters, nor
     women's matters', *Julius Caesar*, I.i, 23

DICK

A plague take you, I thought you did not sneak up and down
after her for nothing. But I prithee tell me, in good sadness,
Robin, is that a conjuring book?

ROBIN

Do but speak what thou'lt have me to do, and I'll do't: if
thou'lt dance naked, put off thy clothes, and I'll conjure thee　　25
about presently; or if thou'lt go but to the tavern with me,
I'll give thee white wine, red wine, claret wine, sack, muscadine, malmsey and whippincrust, hold belly hold, and we'll
not pay one penny for it.

DICK

O brave! Prithee, let's to it presently, for I am as dry as a　　30
dog.

ROBIN

Come then, let's away.　　　　　　　　　　　　*Exeunt*

CHORUS I

Enter the CHORUS

CHORUS

Learned Faustus,
To find the secrets of astronomy,
Graven in the book of Jove's high firmament,
Did mount him up to scale Olympus' top;
Where sitting in a chariot burning bright,　　　　　　　　5
Drawn by the strength of yoked dragons' necks,
He views the clouds, the planets, and the stars,
The tropics, zones, and quarters of the sky,
From the bright circle of the horned moon,
Even to the height of *Primum Mobile:*　　　　　　　　10

22 *in good sadness* seriously
27 *sack* strong, light-coloured wine from Spain
　muscadine muscatel; strong sweet wine from the muscat grape
28 *malmsey* another strong sweet wine
　whippincrust a spiced wine; corruption of hippocras
　hold belly hold a belly-full
7–19 B (*not in A*)
8 *tropics* of Cancer and Capricorn
　zones Four circles (the two tropics and two polar circles) divide
　the world into five zones; this technical word is used by La Pri-
　maudaye (*French Academie*, III, xvii)
9–10 From the innermost to the outermost sphere; everywhere,
　that is, except to the empyrean
10 *Primum Mobile* (see note on II.ii, 35–62)

And whirling round with this circumference,
Within the concave compass of the pole,
From east to west his dragons swiftly glide,
And in eight days did bring him home again.
Not long he stayed within his quiet house,   15
To rest his bones after his weary toil,
But new exploits do hale him out again,
And mounted then upon a dragon's back,
That with his wings did part the subtle air,
He now is gone to prove cosmography,   20
That measures coasts and kingdoms of the earth:
And as I guess will first arrive at Rome,
To see the Pope and manner of his court,
And take some part of holy Peter's feast,
The which this day is highly solemnized.   *Exit*   25

Act III, Scene i

Enter FAUSTUS *and* MEPHOSTOPHILIS

FAUSTUS

Having now, my good Mephostophilis,
Passed with delight the stately town of Trier,
Environed round with airy mountain tops,
With walls of flint, and deep entrenched lakes,
Not to be won by any conquering prince;   5
From Paris next, coasting the realm of France,
We saw the river Main fall into Rhine,
Whose banks are set with groves of fruitful vines.
Then up to Naples, rich Campania,
With buildings fair, and gorgeous to the eye,   10
Whose streets straight forth, and paved with finest brick,
Quarter the town in four equivalents;
There saw we learned Maro's golden tomb,

11 *this circumference* i.e. the Primum Mobile
25 *this day* June 29th is the Feast of St. Peter
 9 *Campania EFB* led Marlowe into this erroneous identification of
    Naples with Campagna
10 *With* ed. (Whose Qq)
11 *Whose* ed. (The Qq)
    straight forth in straight lines
13–15 Virgil (Publius Virgilius Maro) was buried in Naples in 19 B.C.
    and posthumously acquired some reputation as a magician. His
    tomb stands at the end of the promontory of Posilippo between
    Naples and Pozzuoli and legend ascribes the tunnel running
    through this promontory to his magic art.

The way he cut an English mile in length
Thorough a rock of stone in one night's space: 15
From thence to Venice, Padua and the rest,
In midst of which a sumptuous temple stands,
That threats the stars with her aspiring top,
Whose frame is paved with sundry coloured stones,
And roofed aloft with curious work in gold.   20
Thus hitherto hath Faustus spent his time.
But tell me now, what resting place is this?
Hast thou, as erst I did command,
Conducted me within the walls of Rome?

MEPHOSTOPHILIS

I have my Faustus, and for proof thereof,   25
This is the goodly palace of the Pope:
And 'cause we are no common guests,
I choose his privy chamber for our use.

FAUSTUS

I hope his holiness will bid us welcome.

MEPHOSTOPHILIS

All's one, for we'll be bold with his venison.   30
But now my Faustus, that thou may'st perceive,
What Rome contains for to delight thine eyes,
Know that this city stands upon seven hills,
That underprop the groundwork of the same:
Just through the midst runs flowing Tiber's stream,   35
With winding banks that cut it in two parts;
Over the which four stately bridges lean,
That make safe passage to each part of Rome.
Upon the bridge called Ponte Angelo
Erected is a castle passing strong,   40
Where thou shalt see such store of ordinance,
As that the double cannons forged of brass
Do match the number of the days contained
Within the compass of one complete year:

16 *rest* A (east B)
17 *midst* A (one B)
23 *erst* earlier
35–6 B (*not in* A)
42 *double cannons* cannons of very high calibre

17–20 St. Mark's in Venice; details (supplied by *EFB*) of the mosaics
and the gilded roof are accurate, but unless the nearby campanile is
meant the *aspiring top* exists only in the dramatist's imagination. (See
Introduction p. xiv)
39–40 The Ponte Angelo was built in A.D. 135 by Hadrian; his mausoleum
faces the bridge but never stood on it.

Besides the gates, and high pyramides   45
That Julius Caesar brought from Africa.
FAUSTUS
Now by the kingdoms of infernal rule,
Of Styx, of Acheron, and the fiery lake
Of ever-burning Phlegethon, I swear,
That I do long to see the monuments   50
And situation of bright-splendent Rome.
Come therefore, let's away.
MEPHOSTOPHILIS
Nay, stay my Faustus, I know you'd see the Pope,
And take some part of holy Peter's feast,
The which in state and high solemnity,   55
This day is held through Rome and Italy,
In honour of the Pope's triumphant victory.
FAUSTUS
Sweet Mephostophilis, thou pleasest me;
Whilst I am here on earth, let me be cloyed
With all things that delight the heart of man.   60
My four and twenty years of liberty
I'll spend in pleasure and in dalliance,
That Faustus' name, whilst this bright frame doth stand,
May be admired through the furthest land.
MEPHOSTOPHILIS
'Tis well said Faustus, come then stand by me   65
And thou shalt see them come immediately.
FAUSTUS
Nay stay my gentle Mephostophilis,
And grant me my request, and then I go.
Thou knowest within the compass of eight days,
We viewed the face of heaven, of earth and hell: 70

51 *situation* lay-out
55 *in state and* B₂ (this day with B₁)
64 *admired* wondered at

45–6 *pyramides . . . Africa* the obelisk; in fact this was brought from Helio-
    polis by the Emperor Caligula in the first century A.D. The plural form
    pyramides (here stressing the need to pronounce the final syllable) is
    also used as a singular by Marlowe in *The Massacre at Paris*, ii, 43–6.
57 *victory* This must be the victory over Bruno the usurper; but no addi-
    tional pretext should be needed for a feast on St. Peter's day. A reads
    simply:
        Where thou shalt see a troup of bald-pate friars,
        Whose *summum bonum* is in belly-cheer.
    There are only the vestiges of a banquet scene in A.

So high our dragons soared into the air,
That, looking down, the earth appeared to me
No bigger than my hand in quantity.
There did we view the kingdoms of the world,
And what might please mine eye, I there beheld.   75
Then in this show let me an actor be,
That this proud Pope may Faustus' cunning see.

MEPHOSTOPHILIS

Let it be so my Faustus, but first stay,
And view their triumphs, as they pass this way;
And then devise what best contents thy mind,   80
By cunning in thine art to cross the Pope,
Or dash the pride of this solemnity;
To make his monks and abbots stand like apes,
And point like antics at his triple crown:
To beat the beads about the friars' pates,   85
Or clap huge horns upon the cardinals' heads:
Or any villainy thou canst devise,
And I'll perform it Faustus: hark, they come:
This day shall make thee be admired in Rome.

Enter the CARDINALS *and* BISHOPS, *some bearing crosiers, some the
pillars;* MONKS *and* FRIARS *singing their procession: Then the*
POPE, *and* RAYMOND King of Hungary, *with* BRUNO *led in chains*

POPE

Cast down our footstool.

RAYMOND   Saxon Bruno stoop,   90
Whilst on thy back his holiness ascends
Saint Peter's chair and state pontifical.

BRUNO

Proud Lucifer, that state belongs to me:
But thus I fall to Peter, not to thee.

POPE

To me and Peter shalt thou grovelling lie,   95
And crouch before the papal dignity:
Sound trumpets then, for thus Saint Peter's heir,
From Bruno's back ascends Saint Peter's chair.
                    A Flourish while he ascends

77 *cunning* B₄ (coming B₁)
79 *triumphs* procession
81 *cunning* B₄ (coming B₁)
84 *antics* clowns
89 s.d. *pillars* Wolsey substituted portable pillars for the silver
maces usually carried by cardinals
procession office sung in a religious procession

Thus, as the gods creep on with feet of wool,
Long ere with iron hands they punish men,   100
So shall our sleeping vengeance now arise,
And smite with death thy hated enterprise.
Lord Cardinals of France and Padua,
Go forthwith to our holy consistory,
And read amongst the statutes decretal,   105
What by the holy council held at Trent,
The sacred synod hath decreed for him
That doth assume the papal government,
Without election and a true consent:
Away, and bring us word with speed.   110

1 CARDINAL
  We go my Lord.

Exeunt CARDINALS

POPE
  Lord Raymond!
          [*The* POPE *and* RAYMOND *converse*]

FAUSTUS
  Go, haste thee gentle Mephostophilis,
  Follow the cardinals to the consistory;
  And as they turn their superstitious books,   115
  Strike them with sloth, and drowsy idleness;
  And make them sleep so sound, that in their shapes,
  Thyself and I may parley with this Pope,
  This proud confronter of the Emperor,
  And in despite of all his holiness   120
  Restore this Bruno to his liberty,
  And bear him to the states of Germany.

MEPHOSTOPHILIS
  Faustus, I go.

FAUSTUS   Dispatch it soon:
  The Pope shall curse that Faustus came to Rome.

Exeunt FAUSTUS *and* MEPHOSTOPHILIS

BRUNO
  Pope Adrian, let me have some right of law: 125
  I was elected by the Emperor.

POPE
  We will depose the Emperor for that deed,

99–100 Proverb: 'God comes with leaden (woolen) feet but strikes
    with iron hands' (Tilley, G 270)
104 *consistory* meeting place of the papal senate
106 The Council of Trent met, with interruptions, between 1545 and
    1563
107 *synod* general council

And curse the people that submit to him;
Both he and thou shalt stand excommunicate,
And interdict from Church's privilege,   130
And all society of holy men:
He grows too proud in his authority,
Lifting his lofty head above the clouds,
And like a steeple overpeers the Church.
But we'll pull down his haughty insolence;   135
And as Pope Alexander, our progenitor,
Trod on the neck of German Frederick,
Adding this golden sentence to our praise:
That Peter's heirs should tread on emperors,
And walk upon the dreadful adder's back,   140
Treading the lion, and the dragon down,
And fearless spurn the killing basilisk:
So will we quell that haughty schismatic,
And by authority apostolical
Depose him from his regal government.   145

BRUNO

Pope Julius swore to princely Sigismund,
For him, and the succeeding popes of Rome,
To hold the emperors their lawful lords.

POPE

Pope Julius did abuse the Church's rites,
And therefore none of his decrees can stand.   150
Is not all power on earth bestowed on us?
And therefore though we would we cannot err.
Behold this silver belt, whereto is fixed
Seven golden keys fast sealed with seven seals,
In token of our seven-fold power from heaven,   155
To bind or loose, lock fast, condemn, or judge,
Resign, or seal, or whatso pleaseth us.
Then he, and thou, and all the world shall stoop,
Or be assured of our dreadful curse,
To light as heavy as the pains of hell.   160

Enter FAUSTUS *and* MEPHOSTOPHILIS
like the cardinals

---

130 *interdict* officially debarred
136 *progenitor* predecessor
136–7 Pope Alexander III (1159–81) compelled the Emperor
     Frederick Barbarossa to accept his supremacy
142 *basilisk* a mythical beast whose glance was fatal
154 *keys* ed. (seals B) symbolic of St. Peter's keys
157 *Resign* Unseal; the word has the force of Latin *resignare*

MEPHOSTOPHILIS
    Now tell me Faustus, are we not fitted well?
FAUSTUS
    Yes Mephostophilis, and two such cardinals
    Ne'er served a holy pope as we shall do.
    But whilst they sleep within the consistory,
    Let us salute his reverend Fatherhood.   165
RAYMOND
    Behold my Lord, the cardinals are returned.
POPE
    Welcome grave fathers, answer presently,
    What have our holy council there decreed
    Concerning Bruno and the Emperor,
    In quittance of their late conspiracy   170
    Against our state, and papal dignity?
FAUSTUS
    Most sacred patron of the Church of Rome,
    By full consent of all the synod
    Of priests and prelates, it is thus decreed:
    That Bruno and the German Emperor   175
    Be held as lollards and bold schismatics,
    And proud disturbers of the Church's peace.
    And if that Bruno by his own assent,
    Without enforcement of the German peers,
    Did seek to wear the triple diadem,   180
    And by your death to climb Saint Peter's chair,
    The statutes decretal have thus decreed,
    He shall be straight condemned of heresy,
    And on a pile of faggots burnt to death.
POPE
    It is enough: here, take him to your charge,   185
    And bear him straight to Ponte Angelo,
    And in the strongest tower enclose him fast.
    Tomorrow, sitting in our consistory,
    With all our college of grave cardinals,
    We will determine of his life or death.   190
    Here, take his triple crown along with you,
    And leave it in the Church's treasury.
    Make haste again, my good lord cardinals,
    And take our blessing apostolical.

176 *lollards* heretics; originally followers of Wyclif
179 *enforcement of* compulsion from
189 *college* official title for the body of cardinals forming the pope's
    council

MEPHOSTOPHILIS
So, so, was never devil thus blessed before!   195
FAUSTUS
Away sweet Mephostophilis, be gone,
The cardinals will be plagued for this anon.
Exeunt FAUSTUS *and* MEPHOSTOPHILIS [*with* BRUNO]
POPE
Go presently, and bring a banquet forth,
That we may solemnize Saint Peter's feast,
And with Lord Raymond, King of Hungary,   200
Drink to our late and happy victory.   *Exeunt*

Act III, Scene ii

A Sennet while the Banquet is brought in; and then enter
FAUSTUS *and* MEPHOSTOPHILIS
in their own shapes

MEPHOSTOPHILIS
Now Faustus come, prepare thyself for mirth,
The sleepy cardinals are hard at hand,
To censure Bruno, that is posted hence,
And on a proud-paced steed, as swift as thought,
Flies o'er the Alps to fruitful Germany,   5
There to salute the woeful Emperor.
FAUSTUS
The Pope will curse them for their sloth today,
That slept both Bruno and his crown away.
But now, that Faustus may delight his mind,
And by their folly make some merriment,   10
Sweet Mephostophilis, so charm me here,
That I may walk invisible to all,
And do whate'er I please, unseen of any.
MEPHOSTOPHILIS
Faustus thou shalt, then kneel down presently:
Whilst on thy head I lay my hand,   15
And charm thee with this magic wand:
First wear this girdle, then appear
Invisible to all are here:
The planets seven, the gloomy air,

s.d. *Sennet* A flourish on the trumpets, usually heralding a ceremonious
    entrance

> *Hell, and the Furies' forked hair,* 20
> *Pluto's blue fire, and Hecat's tree,*
> *With magic spells so compass thee,*
> *That no eye may thy body see.*

So Faustus, now for all their holiness,
Do what thou wilt, thou shalt not be discerned. 25

FAUSTUS

Thanks Mephostophilis: now friars take heed,
Lest Faustus make your shaven crowns to bleed.

MEPHOSTOPHILIS

Faustus no more: see where the cardinals come.

Sound a sennet. Enter POPE *and all the* LORDS
Enter the CARDINALS *with a book*

POPE

Welcome Lord Cardinals: come sit down.
Lord Raymond, take your seat. Friars attend, 30
And see that all things be in readiness,
As best beseems this solemn festival.

1 CARDINAL

First, may it please your sacred Holiness,
To view the sentence of the reverend synod,
Concerning Bruno and the Emperor? 35

POPE

What needs this question? Did I not tell you,
Tomorrow we would sit i'th'consistory,
And there determine of his punishment?
You brought us word even now, it was decreed,
That Bruno and the cursed Emperor 40
Were by the holy council both condemned
For loathed lollards and base schismatics:
Then wherefore would you have me view that book?

1 CARDINAL

Your Grace mistakes; you gave us no such charge.

POPE

Deny it not, we all are witnesses 45
That Bruno here was late delivered you
With his rich triple crown to be reserved,
And put into the Church's treasury.

20 *forked hair* the forked tongues of the snakes which form the hair of the
Furies
21 *Pluto's blue fire* the sulphurous smoke of hell
Hecat's tree perhaps the gallows tree, since Hecate was also Trivia,
goddess of cross-roads where the gallows was set up. Boas may be
right in thinking that *tree* ought to be *three*, in allusion to the triple form
of the deity (Luna in Heaven, Diana on Earth and Hecate or Proserpina
in Hell).

AMBO CARDINALS

By holy Paul we saw them not.

POPE

By Peter, you shall die,　　　　　　　　　　　　　50
Unless you bring them forth immediately:
Hale them to prison, lade their limbs with gyves:
False prelates, for this hateful treachery,
Cursed be your souls to hellish misery.

　　　　　　　[Exeunt CARDINALS *with some* FRIARS]

FAUSTUS

So, they are safe: now Faustus, to the feast;　　　55
The Pope had never such a frolic guest.

POPE

Lord Archbishop of Rheims, sit down with us.

ARCHBISHOP

I thank your Holiness.

FAUSTUS

Fall to! The devil choke you an you spare.

POPE

Who's that spoke? Friars, look about!　　　　　60
Lord Raymond, pray fall to; I am beholding
To the Bishop of Milan, for this so rare a present.

FAUSTUS

I thank you sir.　　　　　　　　　　　*Snatch it*

POPE

How now? Who snatched the meat from me?
Villains, why speak you not?　　　　　　　　65
My good Lord Archbishop, here's a most dainty dish,
Was sent me from a cardinal in France.

FAUSTUS

I'll have that too.　　　　　　　　　*[Snatch it]*

POPE

What lollards do attend our Holiness,
That we receive such great indignity?　　　　70
Fetch me some wine.

FAUSTUS

Ay, pray do, for Faustus is a-dry.

POPE

Lord Raymond, I drink unto your grace.

FAUSTUS

I pledge your grace.　　　　　　　　*[Snatch cup]*

POPE

My wine gone too! Ye lubbers, look about　　　75

49 *Ambo* Both

And find the man that doth this villainy,
Or by our sanctitude you all shall die.
I pray my lords have patience at this troublesome banquet.

ARCHBISHOP

Please it your Holiness, I think it be some ghost crept out of
purgatory, and now is come unto your Holiness for his   80
pardon.

POPE

It may be so:
Go then command our priests to sing a dirge,
To lay the fury of this same troublesome ghost.
Once again my lord, fall to.   85

The POPE *crosseth himself*

FAUSTUS

How now? Must every bit be spiced with a cross?
Nay then, take that.

FAUSTUS *hits him a box of the ear*

POPE

O, I am slain! Help me my lords!
O come and help to bear my body hence:
Damned be this soul for ever for this deed.   90

Exeunt the POPE *and his train*

MEPHOSTOPHILIS

Now Faustus, what will you do now? For I can tell you,
you'll be cursed with bell, book and candle.

FAUSTUS

Bell, book and candle; candle, book and bell,
Forward and backward, to curse Faustus to hell.

Enter the FRIARS *with Bell, Book and Candle for the Dirge*

---

83 *dirge* corruption of *dirige*, the antiphon at Matins in the Office for
the dead, hence any requiem mass; correctly used here but not
at line 102 below

86–7 The A pope is allowed to cross himself three times, with a warning
from Faustus on each occasion:

> *The Pope crosseth himself*
> What, are you crossing of yourself?
> Well, use that trick no more, I would advise you.
> *Cross again*
> Well, there's the second time; aware the third,
> I give you fair warning.
> *Cross again, and* FAUSTUS *hits him a box of the ear*

This sounds to me like a comedian's expansion.

1 FRIAR

    Come brethren, let's about our business with good devotion.   95
                                 Sing this
      Cursed be he that stole his Holiness' meat from the table.
        Maledicat Dominus.
      Cursed be he that struck his Holiness a blow on the face.
        Maledicat Dominus.
      Cursed be he that took Friar Sandelo a blow on the pate.   100
        Maledicat Dominus.
      Cursed be he that disturbeth our holy dirge.
        Maledicat Dominus.
      Cursed be he that took away his Holiness' wine.
        Maledicat Dominus   105
      [FAUSTUS *and* MEPHOSTOPHILIS] *beat the* FRIARS, *fling*
        fireworks among them, and Exeunt

Act III, Scene iii

Enter CLOWN [ROBIN] *and* DICK, *with a Cup*

DICK

    Sirra Robin, we were best look that your devil can answer
    the stealing of this same cup, for the vintner's boy follows
    us at the hard heels.

ROBIN

    'Tis no matter, let him come; an he follow us, I'll so conjure
    him, as he was never conjured in his life, I warrant him: let   5
    me see the cup.

Enter VINTNER

DICK

    Here 'tis–yonder he comes! Now Robin, now or never show
    thy cunning.

VINTNER

    O, are you here? I am glad I have found you. You are a
    couple of fine companions! Pray, where's the cup you stole   10
    from the tavern?

---

 97 *Maledicat Dominus* May the Lord curse him
III,iii. A's version of this scene is printed in the Appendix (p. 91)
  3 *at the hard heels* close on our heels

---

106 A concludes the scene with the formal '*Et omnes sancti, Amen*' (and all
    the saints, Amen). From lines 100 and 102, however, it seems that
    Faustus is making a nuisance of himself; this and the stage direction
    suggests that the scene comes to a sharp and undignified end.

ROBIN

How, how? We steal a cup! Take heed what you say; we look
not like cup-stealers, I can tell you.

VINTNER

Never deny't, for I know you have it, and I'll search you.

ROBIN

Search me? Ay, and spare not—hold the cup Dick—come,   15
come, search me, search me.

[VINTNER *searches* ROBIN]

VINTNER

Come on sirra, let me search you now.

DICK

Ay, ay, do, do—hold the cup Robin—I fear not your search-
ing; we scorn to steal your cups, I can tell you.

[VINTNER *searches* DICK]

VINTNER

Never outface me for the matter, for sure the cup is between   20
you two.

ROBIN

Nay, there you lie, 'tis beyond us both.

VINTNER

A plague take you, I thought 'twas your knavery to take it
away. Come, give it me again.

ROBIN

Ay much! When, can you tell? Dick, make me a circle, and   25
stand close at my back, and stir not for thy life. Vintner,
you shall have your cup anon—say nothing Dick! *O per se,
o; Demogorgon, Belcher and Mephostophilis!*

Enter MEPHOSTOPHILIS

MEPHOSTOPHILIS

You princely legions of infernal rule,
How am I vexed by these villains' charms!   30
From Constantinople have they brought me now,
Only for pleasure of these damned slaves.

[*Exit* VINTNER]

ROBIN

By lady sir, you have had a shrewd journey of it. Will it

---

20 *outface . . . matter* brazen it out with me
22 *beyond us both* out of our hands; the Clowns have succeeded in
   juggling with the cup so that neither holds it
25 *Ay . . . tell* derisive comments
33 *shrewd* tiresome

please you to take a shoulder of mutton to supper, and a
tester in your purse, and go back again?   35

DICK

Ay, I pray you heartily sir, for we called you but in jest, I
promise you.

MEPHOSTOPHILIS

To purge the rashness of this cursed deed,
First, be thou turned to this ugly shape,
For apish deeds transformed to an ape.   40

ROBIN

O brave, an ape! I pray sir, let me have the carrying of him
about to show some tricks.

MEPHOSTOPHILIS

And so thou shalt: be thou transformed to a dog, and carry
him upon thy back. Away, be gone!

ROBIN

A dog? That's excellent: let the maids look well to their   45
porridge-pots, for I'll into the kitchen presently: come
Dick, come.

Exeunt the two CLOWNS

MEPHOSTOPHILIS

Now with the flames of ever-burning fire,
I'll wing myself, and forthwith fly amain
Unto my Faustus, to the great Turk's court.   *Exit*   50

CHORUS 2

Enter CHORUS

CHORUS

When Faustus had with pleasure ta'en the view
Of rarest things and royal courts of kings,
He stayed his course, and so returned home,
Where such as bare his absence but with grief—
I mean his friends and near'st companions—   5
Did gratulate his safety with kind words;
And in their conference of what befell,
Touching his journey through the world and air,
They put forth questions of astrology,
Which Faustus answered with such learned skill,   10
As they admired and wondered at his wit.
Now is his fame spread forth in every land:

35 *tester* sixpence; a slang term

Chorus 2 Not to be found in B, this Chorus preceded the Clowns' scene
     with the goblet in A

Amongst the rest, the Emperor is one,
Carolus the fifth, at whose palace now
Faustus is feasted 'mongst his noblemen.   15
What there he did in trial of his art,
I leave untold, your eyes shall see performed.

Act IV, Scene i

Enter MARTINO *and* FREDERICK *at several doors*

MARTINO
What ho, officers, gentlemen,
Hie to the presence to attend the Emperor!
Good Frederick, see the rooms be voided straight,
His Majesty is coming to the hall;
Go back, and see the state in readiness.   5
FREDERICK
But where is Bruno, our elected Pope,
That on a fury's back came post from Rome?
Will not his grace consort the Emperor?
MARTINO
O yes, and with him comes the German conjuror,
The learned Faustus, fame of Wittenberg,   10
The wonder of the world for magic art;
And he intends to show great Carolus,
The race of all his stout progenitors;
And bring in presence of his Majesty,
The royal shapes and warlike semblances   15
Of Alexander and his beauteous paramour.
FREDERICK
Where is Benvolio?
MARTINO
Fast asleep I warrant you.
He took his rouse with stoups of Rhenish wine
So kindly yesternight to Bruno's health,   20
That all this day the sluggard keeps his bed.
FREDERICK
See, see, his window's ope; we'll call to him.

14 *Carolus* Charles V, Emperor 1519–56
 2 *presence* audience chamber
 3 *voided straight* cleared instantly
 5 *state* throne
15 *warlike* heroic
19 *took his rouse* had a heavy drinking session; *cf. Hamlet*, I.iv, 8–10
   stoups measures

MARTINO
    What ho, Benvolio!

> *Enter* BENVOLIO *above at a window, in his nightcap;*
> *buttoning*

BENVOLIO
    What a devil ail you two?
MARTINO
    Speak softly sir, lest the devil hear you: 25
    For Faustus at the court is late arrived,
    And at his heels a thousand furies wait,
    To accomplish whatsoever the doctor please.
BENVOLIO
    What of this?
MARTINO
    Come, leave thy chamber first, and thou shalt see   30
    This conjuror perform such rare exploits,
    Before the Pope and royal Emperor,
    As never yet was seen in Germany.
BENVOLIO
    Has not the Pope enough of conjuring yet?
    He was upon the devil's back late enough;   35
    And if he be so far in love with him
    I would he would post with him to Rome again.
FREDERICK
    Speak, wilt thou come and see this sport?
BENVOLIO
    Not I.
MARTINO
    Wilt thou stand in thy window, and see it then?   40
BENVOLIO
    Ay, and I fall not asleep i'th'meantime.
MARTINO
    The Emperor is at hand, who comes to see
    What wonders by black spells may compassed be.
BENVOLIO
    Well, go you attend the Emperor; I am content for this
    once to thrust my head out at a window: for they say, if a   45
    man be drunk overnight, the devil cannot hurt him in the
    morning: if that be true, I have a charm in my head, shall
    control him as well as the conjuror, I warrant you.
                            [*Exeunt* FREDERICK *and* MARTINO]

23 **s. d.** *buttoning* buttoning up his clothes; the intransitive use of
the verb is rare

Act IV, Scene ii

A Sennet. CHARLES *the* GERMAN EMPEROR, BRUNO,
SAXONY, FAUSTUS, MEPHOSTOPHILIS, FREDERICK, MARTINO,
and ATTENDANTS
[BENVOLIO *remains in the window*]

EMPEROR

Wonder of men, renowned magician,
Thrice-learned Faustus, welcome to our court.
This deed of thine, in setting Bruno free
From his and our professed enemy,
Shall add more excellence unto thine art,   5
Than if by powerful necromantic spells,
Thou could'st command the world's obedience:
For ever be beloved of Carolus.
And if this Bruno thou hast late redeemed,
In peace possess the triple diadem,   10
And sit in Peter's chair, despite of chance,
Thou shalt be famous through all Italy,
And honoured of the German Emperor.

FAUSTUS

These gracious words, most royal Carolus,
Shall make poor Faustus to his utmost power,   15
Both love and serve the German Emperor,
And lay his life at holy Bruno's feet.
For proof whereof, if so your grace be pleased,
The doctor stands prepared, by power of art,
To cast his magic charms, that shall pierce through   20
The ebon gates of ever-burning hell,
And hale the stubborn furies from their caves,
To compass whatsoe'er your grace commands.

BENVOLIO

'Blood, he speaks terribly; but for all that, I do not greatly
believe him; he looks as like a conjuror as the Pope to a   25
costermonger.

EMPEROR

Then Faustus, as thou late didst promise us,
We would behold that famous conqueror,
Great Alexander, and his paramour,
In their true shapes, and state majestical,   30
That we may wonder at their excellence.

IV.ii. A's version of this scene is printed in the Appendix (p. 93)
  29 *paramour* Alexander's wife, Roxana

FAUSTUS
Your Majesty shall see them presently.
Mephostophilis, away!
And with a solemn noise of trumpets' sound,
Present before this royal Emperor,   35
Great Alexander and his beauteous paramour.
MEPHOSTOPHILIS
Faustus I will.

Exit

BENVOLIO
Well master doctor, an your devils come not away quickly,
you shall have me asleep presently: zounds, I could eat
myself for anger, to think I have been such an ass all this   40
while, to stand gaping after the devil's governor, and can
see nothing.
FAUSTUS
I'll make you feel something anon, if my art fail me not.
My lord, I must forewarn your Majesty,
That when my spirits present the royal shapes   45
Of Alexander and his paramour,
Your grace demand no questions of the king,
But in dumb silence let them come and go.
EMPEROR
Be it as Faustus please, we are content.
BENVOLIO
Ay, ay, and I am content too: and thou bring Alexander and   50
his paramour before the Emperor, I'll be Actaeon, and turn
my self to a stag.
FAUSTUS
And I'll play Diana, and send you the horns presently.
Sennet. Enter at one door the EMPEROR ALEXANDER, *at the other*
DARIUS: *they meet,* DARIUS *is thrown down,* ALEXANDER *kills him;*
takes off his crown, and offering to go out, his PARAMOUR *meets*
him, he embraceth her, and sets DARIUS' *crown upon her head; and*
coming back, both salute the EMPEROR, *who leaving his state,*
offers to embrace them, which FAUSTUS *seeing, suddenly stays him.*
        Then trumpets cease, and music sounds
My gracious lord, you do forget yourself;
These are but shadows, not substantial.   55

44–8 The A Text (see Appendix p. 94) makes it plain that the Emperor is
   to be shown spirits in the forms of Alexander and his paramour—hence
   the need for silence.
51 *Actaeon* As punishment for coming upon Diana and her nymphs
   bathing, Actaeon was turned into a stag, and his own hounds tore
   him to pieces.

EMPEROR

O pardon me, my thoughts are so ravished
With sight of this renowned emperor,
That in mine arms I would have compassed him.
But Faustus, since I may not speak to them,
To satisfy my longing thoughts at full,   60
Let me this tell thee: I have heard it said,
That this fair lady, whilst she lived on earth,
Had on her neck a little wart or mole;
How may I prove that saying to be true?

FAUSTUS

Your Majesty may boldly go and see.   65

EMPEROR

Faustus I see it plain,
And in this sight thou better pleasest me,
Than if I gained another monarchy.

FAUSTUS

Away, be gone.   *Exit* SHOW
See, see, my gracious lord, what strange beast is yon, that 70
thrusts his head out at window?

EMPEROR

O wondrous sight! See, Duke of Saxony,
Two spreading horns most strangely fastened
Upon the head of young Benvolio.

SAXONY

What, is he asleep, or dead?   75

FAUSTUS

He sleeps my lord, but dreams not of his horns.

EMPEROR

This sport is excellent: we'll call and wake him.
What ho, Benvolio!

BENVOLIO

A plague upon you, let me sleep awhile.

EMPEROR

I blame thee not to sleep much, having such a head of thine 80
own.

SAXONY

Look up Benvolio, 'tis the Emperor calls.

BENVOLIO

The Emperor? Where? O zounds my head!

EMPEROR

Nay, and thy horns hold, 'tis no matter for thy head, for
that's armed sufficiently.   85

FAUSTUS

Why, how now sir knight? What, hanged by the horns? This

is most horrible! Fie, fie, pull in your head for shame, let
not all the world wonder at you.

BENVOLIO

Zounds doctor, is this your villainy?

FAUSTUS

O say not so sir: the doctor has no skill,   90
No art, no cunning, to present these lords,
Or bring before this royal Emperor
The mighty monarch, warlike Alexander.
If Faustus do it, you are straight resolved
In bold Actaeon's shape to turn a stag.   95
And therefore my lord, so please your Majesty,
I'll raise a kennel of hounds shall hunt him so,
As all his footmanship shall scarce prevail
To keep his carcase from their bloody fangs.
Ho, Belimote, Argiron, Asterote!   100

BENVOLIO

Hold, hold! Zounds, he'll raise up a kennel of devils, I
think, anon: good my lord, entreat for me: 'sblood, I am
never able to endure these torments.

EMPEROR

Then good master doctor,
Let me entreat you to remove his horns,   105
He has done penance now sufficiently.

FAUSTUS

My gracious lord, not so much for injury done to me, as
to delight your Majesty with some mirth, hath Faustus
justly requited this injurious knight; which being all I
desire, I am content to remove his horns. Mephostophilis,   110
transform him—and hereafter sir, look you speak well of
scholars.

BENVOLIO

Speak well of ye! 'Sblood, and scholars be such cuckold-
makers to clap horns of honest men's heads o' this order,
I'll ne'er trust smooth faces and small ruffs more. But an I be   115
not revenged for this, would I might be turned to a gaping
oyster, and drink nothing but salt water.

EMPEROR

Come Faustus, while the Emperor lives,
In recompense of this thy high desert,
Thou shalt command the state of Germany,   120
And live beloved of mighty Carolus.

Exeunt omnes

98 *footmanship* skill in running
115 *smooth . . . ruffs* beardless scholars in academic dress

Act IV, Scene iii

Enter BENVOLIO, MARTINO, FREDERICK, *and* SOLDIERS

MARTINO
　Nay sweet Benvolio, let us sway thy thoughts
　From this attempt against the conjuror.
BENVOLIO
　Away, you love me not, to urge me thus.
　Shall I let slip so great an injury,
　When every servile groom jests at my wrongs,　　　　　5
　And in their rustic gambols proudly say,
　'Benvolio's head was graced with horns today'?
　O may these eyelids never close again,
　Till with my sword I have that conjuror slain.
　If you will aid me in this enterprise,　　　　　　　10
　Then draw your weapons, and be resolute:
　If not, depart: here will Benvolio die,
　But Faustus' death shall quit my infamy.
FREDERICK
　Nay, we will stay with thee, betide what may,
　And kill that doctor if he come this way.　　　　　　15
BENVOLIO
　Then gentle Frederick, hie thee to the grove,
　And place our servants and our followers
　Close in an ambush there behind the trees.
　By this (I know) the conjuror is near,
　I saw him kneel and kiss the Emperor's hand,　　　　20
　And take his leave, laden with rich rewards.
　Then soldiers boldly fight; if Faustus die,
　Take you the wealth, leave us the victory.
FREDERICK
　Come soldiers, follow me unto the grove;
　Who kills him shall have gold and endless love.　　　25
　　　　　　　　　　　Exit FREDERICK *with the* SOLDIERS
BENVOLIO
　My head is lighter than it was by th'horns,

　6 *proudly* insolently
　13 *But* Unless
　18 *Close* Hidden
　19 *By this* By this time

But yet my heart's more ponderous than my head,
And pants until I see that conjuror dead.
MARTINO
Where shall we place ourselves Benvolio?
BENVOLIO
Here will we stay to bide the first assault.   30
O were that damned hell-hound but in place,
Thou soon should'st see me quit my foul disgrace.

                        Enter FREDERICK

FREDERICK
Close, close, the conjuror is at hand,
And all alone, comes walking in his gown.
Be ready then, and strike the peasant down.   35
BENVOLIO
Mine be that honour then: now sword strike home,
For horns he gave, I'll have his head anon.

              Enter FAUSTUS *with the false head*

MARTINO
See, see, he comes.
BENVOLIO   No words; this blow ends all,
Hell take his soul, his body thus must fall.
                                          [*Strikes* FAUSTUS]
FAUSTUS
O!   40
FREDERICK
Groan you master doctor?
BENVOLIO
Break may his heart with groans: dear Frederick see,
Thus will I end his griefs immediately.
                                          [*Cuts off his head*]
MARTINO
Strike with a willing hand; his head is off.
BENVOLIO
The devil's dead, the furies now may laugh.   45
FREDERICK
Was this that stern aspect, that awful frown,
Made the grim monarch of infernal spirits,
Tremble and quake at his commanding charms?
MARTINO
Was this that damned head, whose heart conspired
Benvolio's shame before the Emperor?   50

31 *in place* on the spot

BENVOLIO

Ay, that's the head, and here the body lies,
Justly rewarded for his villainies.

FREDERICK

Come, let's devise how we may add more shame
To the black scandal of his hated name.

BENVOLIO

First, on his head, in quittance of my wrongs,   55
I'll nail huge forked horns, and let them hang
Within the window where he yoked me first,
That all the world may see my just revenge.

MARTINO

What use shall we put his beard to?

BENVOLIO

We'll sell it to a chimney-sweeper; it will wear out   60
ten birchen brooms, I warrant you.

FREDERICK

What shall eyes do?

BENVOLIO

We'll put out his eyes, and they shall serve for buttons to
his lips, to keep his tongue from catching cold.

MARTINO

An excellent policy: and now sirs, having divided him,   65
what shall the body do?   [FAUSTUS *stands up*]

BENVOLIO

Zounds, the devil's alive again!

FREDERICK

Give him his head for God's sake.

FAUSTUS

Nay keep it: Faustus will have heads and hands,
Ay, all your hearts to recompense this deed.   70
Knew you not, traitors, I was limited
For four and twenty years to breathe on earth?
And had you cut my body with your swords,
Or hewed this flesh and bones as small as sand,
Yet in a minute had my spirit returned,   75
And I had breathed a man made free from harm.
But wherefore do I dally my revenge?
Asteroth, Belimoth, Mephostophilis!

Enter MEPHOSTOPHILIS *and other* DEVILS

Go, horse these traitors on your fiery backs,
And mount aloft with them as high as heaven,   80

70 *Ay, all* ed. (I call B)

Thence pitch them headlong to the lowest hell:
Yet stay, the world shall see their misery,
And hell shall after plague their treachery.
Go Belimoth, and take this caitiff hence,
And hurl him in some lake of mud and dirt: 85
Take thou this other, drag him through the woods,
Amongst the pricking thorns and sharpest briers,
Whilst with my gentle Mephostophilis,
This traitor flies unto some steepy rock,
That, rolling down, may break the villain's bones,   90
As he intended to dismember me.
Fly hence, dispatch my charge immediately.

FREDERICK

Pity us gentle Faustus, save our lives.

FAUSTUS

Away!

FREDERICK

He must needs go that the devil drives.   95

Exeunt SPIRITS *with the* KNIGHTS

Enter the ambushed SOLDIERS

1 SOLDIER

Come sirs, prepare yourselves in readiness,
Make haste to help these noble gentlemen;
I heard them parley with the conjuror.

2 SOLDIER

See where he comes, dispatch, and kill the slave.

FAUSTUS

What's here? An ambush to betray my life!   100
Then Faustus try thy skill: base pcasants stand!
For lo, these trees remove at my command,
And stand as bulwarks 'twixt yourselves and me,
To shield me from your hated treachery:
Yet to encounter this your weak attempt,   105
Behold an army comes incontinent.

FAUSTUS *strikes the door, and enter a* DEVIL *playing on a drum,
after him another bearing an ensign: and divers with weapons,*
MEPHOSTOPHILIS *with fireworks; they set upon the* SOLDIERS
and drive them out

[*Exit* FAUSTUS]

95 A well known proverb (Tilley, D 278)
106 *incontinent* without delay

Act IV, Scene iv

Enter at several doors, BENVOLIO, FREDERICK, *and* MARTINO,
their heads and faces bloody, and besmeared with mud and dirt;
all having horns on their heads

MARTINO
What ho, Benvolio!
BENVOLIO
Here, what Frederick, ho!
FREDERICK
O help me gentle friend; where is Martino?
MARTINO
Dear Frederick here,
Half smothered in a lake of mud and dirt,   5
Through which the furies dragged me by the heels.
FREDERICK
Martino see, Benvolio's horns again!
MARTINO
O misery! How now, Benvolio?
BENVOLIO
Defend me heaven! Shall I be haunted still?
MARTINO
Nay, fear not man, we have no power to kill.   10
BENVOLIO
My friends transformed thus! O hellish spite,
Your heads are all set with horns.
FREDERICK   You hit it right,
It is your own you mean; feel on your head.
BENVOLIO
Zounds, horns again!
MARTINO   Nay, chafe not man, we all are sped.
BENVOLIO
What devil attends this damned magician,   15
That spite of spite, our wrongs are doubled?
FREDERICK
What may we do, that we may hide our shame?
BENVOLIO
If we should follow him to work revenge,
He'd join long asses' ears to these huge horns,
And make us laughing-stocks to all the world.   20
MARTINO
What shall we do then dear Benvolio?

10 *kill* This suggests a pun on *haunted/hunted* in the preceding line

BENVOLIO
I have a castle joining near these woods,
And thither we'll repair and live obscure,
Till time shall alter these our brutish shapes:
Sith black disgrace hath thus eclipsed our fame,   25
We'll rather die with grief, than live with shame.

Exeunt omnes

Act IV, Scene v

Enter FAUSTUS *and the* HORSE-COURSER

HORSE-COURSER
I beseech your worship accept of these forty dollars.
FAUSTUS
Friend, thou canst not buy so good a horse for so small a
price: I have no great need to sell him, but if thou likest
him for ten dollars more, take him, because I can see thou
hast a good mind to him.   5
HORSE-COURSER
I beseech you sir, accept of this; I am a very poor man, and
have lost very much of late by horse-flesh, and this bargain
will set me up again.
FAUSTUS
Well, I will not stand with thee; give me the money. Now,
sirra, I must tell you, that you may ride him o'er hedge and   10
ditch, and spare him not; but: do you hear, in any case ride
him not into the water.
HORSE-COURSER
How sir, not into the water? Why, will he not drink of all
waters?
FAUSTUS
Yes, he will drink of all waters, but ride him not into the   15

24 *Till time shall alter EFB* explains that the knights were condemned
     to wear the horns for a month
26 'It is better to die with honour than live with shame' (Tilley,
     H 576)
IV.v. A's version of this scene is printed in the Appendix (p. 96)
s.d. *Horse-courser* Horse-dealer; a reputation for dishonesty has always
     attached to such traders
 9 *stand with thee* haggle over it
11 *in any case* whatever happens
12 *not into the water* Running water (but not the stagnant water of a
     ditch) dissolves a witch's spell
13–14 *drink of all waters* go anywhere; 'I am for all waters', *Twelfth
     Night*, IV.ii, 57

water; o'er hedge and ditch, or where thou wilt, but not
into the water. Go bid the ostler deliver him unto you, and
remember what I say.

HORSE-COURSER

I warrant you sir; O joyful day! Now am I a made man for
ever. *Exit* 20

FAUSTUS

What art thou, Faustus, but a man condemned to die?
Thy fatal time draws to a final end;
Despair doth drive distrust into my thoughts.
Confound these passions with a quiet sleep:
Tush, Christ did call the thief upon the cross; 25
Then rest thee, Faustus, quiet in conceit.

He sits to sleep

Enter the HORSE-COURSER, *wet*

HORSE-COURSER

O what a cozening doctor was this! I riding my horse into
the water, thinking some hidden mystery had been in the
horse, I had nothing under me but a little straw, and had
much ado to escape drowning. Well, I'll go rouse him, and 30
make him give me my forty dollars again. Ho, sirra doctor,
you cozening scab! Maister doctor awake, and rise, and give
me my money again, for your horse is turned to a bottle of
hay. Maister doctor—

He pulls off his leg

Alas, I am undone, what shall I do? I have pulled off his leg! 35

FAUSTUS

O help, help, the villain hath murdered me!

HORSE-COURSER

Murder or not murder, now he has but one leg, I'll out-run
him, and cast this leg into some ditch or other. *[Exit]*

FAUSTUS

Stop him, stop him, stop him!—ha, ha, ha, Faustus hath
his leg again, and the horse-courser a bundle of hay for his 40
forty dollars.

Enter WAGNER

How now Wagner, what news with thee?

26 *in conceit* in this thought
27 *cozening* cheating
32 *Maister* Here, and in the succeeding comic scenes, the author
attempts to indicate dialectal pronunciation
33 *bottle* truss

WAGNER

If it please you, the Duke of Vanholt doth earnestly entreat your company, and hath sent some of his men to
attend you with provision fit for your journey.   45

FAUSTUS

The Duke of Vanholt's an honourable gentleman, and one
to whom I must be no niggard of my cunning. Come away.

Exeunt

Act IV, Scene vi

Enter CLOWN [ROBIN], DICK,
HORSE-COURSER, *and a* CARTER

CARTER

Come my masters, I'll bring you to the best beer in Europe.
What ho hostess! Where be these whores?

Enter HOSTESS

HOSTESS

How now, what lack you? What, my old guests, welcome.

ROBIN

Sirra Dick, dost thou know why I stand so mute?

DICK

No Robin, why is't?   5

ROBIN

I am eighteenpence on the score; but say nothing, see if she
have forgotten me.

HOSTESS

Who's this, that stands so solemnly by himself? What, my
old guest!

ROBIN

O hostess, how do you? I hope my score stands still.   10

HOSTESS

Ay, there's no doubt of that, for methinks you make no
haste to wipe it out.

DICK

Why hostess, I say, fetch us some beer.

HOSTESS

You shall presently. Look up into th'hall there, ho!   *Exit*

---

2 *whores* 'A cup of ale without a wench, why alas, 'tis like an egg
   without salt, or a red herring without mustard', *Looking Glass for London*, II,278–80
14 *Look . . . ho* The Hostess calls to her servants

DICK

Come sirs, what shall we do now till mine hostess comes?   15

CARTER

Marry sir, I'll tell you the bravest tale how a conjuror served me; you know Doctor Fauster?

HORSE-COURSER

Ay, a plague take him. Here's some on's have cause to know him. Did he conjure thee too?

CARTER

I'll tell you how he served me. As I was going to Wittenberg   20
t'other day, with a load of hay, he met me, and asked me what he should give me for as much hay as he could eat. Now, sir, I, thinking that a little would serve his turn, bade him take as much as he would for three farthings. So he presently gave me my money, and fell to eating, and as I am   25
a cursen man, he never left eating, till he had eat up all my load of hay.

ALL

O monstrous, eat a whole load of hay!

ROBIN

Yes, yes, that may be; for I have heard of one, that h'as eat a load of logs.   30

HORSE-COURSER

Now sirs, you shall hear how villainously he served me: I went to him yesterday to buy a horse of him, and he would by no means sell him under forty dollars; so sir, because I knew him to be such a horse, as would run over hedge and ditch, and never tire, I gave him his money. So when I had   35
my horse, Doctor Fauster bade me ride him night and day, and spare him no time; 'But', quoth he, 'in any case ride him not into the water'. Now sir, I, thinking the horse had had some quality that he would not have me know of, what did I but rid him into a great river, and when I came just in   40
the midst, my horse vanished away, and I sat straddling upon a bottle of hay.

ALL

O brave doctor!

HORSE-COURSER

But you shall hear how bravely I served him for it. I went me home to his house, and there I found him asleep; I kept   45
a-hallowing and whooping in his ears, but all could not wake him. I, seeing that, took him by the leg, and never

26 *cursen* Christian; the dialectal form of christened
29 *h'as* he has

rested pulling, till I had pulled me his leg quite off, and
now 'tis at home in mine hostry.

ROBIN

And has the doctor but one leg then? That's excellent, for   50
one of his devils turned me into the likeness of an ape's face.

CARTER

Some more drink hostess!

ROBIN

Hark you, we'll into another room and drink awhile, and
then we'll go seek out the doctor.

Exeunt omnes

Act IV, Scene vii

Enter the DUKE OF VANHOLT, *his* DUCHESS,
FAUSTUS, *and* MEPHOSTOPHILIS

DUKE

Thanks master doctor, for these pleasant sights. Nor know
I how sufficiently to recompense your great deserts in erect-
ing that enchanted castle in the air; the sight whereof so
delighted me, as nothing in the world could please me more.

FAUSTUS

I do think myself, my good lord, highly recompensed in   5
that it pleaseth your grace to think but well of that which
Faustus hath performed. But gracious lady, it may be that
you have taken no pleasure in those sights; therefore I pray
you tell me, what is the thing you most desire to have: be
it in the world, it shall be yours. I have heard that great-   10
bellied women do long for things are rare and dainty.

LADY

True, master doctor, and since I find you so kind, I will
make known unto you what my heart desires to have; and
were it now summer, as it is January, a dead time of the
winter, I would request no better meat, than a dish of ripe   15
grapes.

FAUSTUS

This is but a small matter: go Mephostophilis, away.

Exit MEPHOSTOPHILIS

Madam, I will do more than this for your content.

Enter MEPHOSTOPHILIS *again with the grapes*

IV.vii. A's version of this scene does not include the intrusion of the
   Clowns (32 ff)

Here, now taste ye these; they should be good for they
come from a far country, I can tell you.   20

DUKE

This makes me wonder more than all the rest, that at this
time of the year, when every tree is barren of his fruits,
from whence you had these ripe grapes.

FAUSTUS

Please it your grace, the year is divided into two circles over
the whole world, so that when it is winter with us, in the   25
contrary circle it is likewise summer with them, as in
India, Saba, and such countries that lie far east, where they
have fruit twice a year. From whence, by means of a swift
spirit that I have, I had these grapes brought as you see.

LADY

And trust me, they are the sweetest grapes that e'er I   30
tasted.

                The CLOWNS *bounce at the gate, within*

DUKE

What rude disturbers have we at the gate?
Go pacify their fury, set it ope,
And then demand of them, what they would have.

          They knock again, and call out to talk with FAUSTUS

A SERVANT

Why, how now masters? What a coil is there! What is   35
the reason you disturb the Duke?

DICK

We have no reason for it, therefore a fig for him.

SERVANT

Why saucy varlets, dare you be so bold?

HORSE-COURSER

I hope sir, we have wit enough to be more bold than
welcome.   40

SERVANT

It appears so; pray be bold elsewhere, and trouble not the
Duke.

DUKE

What would they have?

24–8 The relevant circles would be the northern and southern hemi-
    spheres, but the author appears to be thinking in terms of east
    and west; *EFB* evades the matter while providing the detail of
    the twice-yearly fruit
27 *Saba* Sheba
31 s.d. *bounce* beat
35 *coil* din
37 *reason . . . fig* Dick makes the not uncommon pun on reason/raisin

SERVANT

    They all cry out to speak with Doctor Faustus.

CARTER

    Ay, and we will speak with him.   45

DUKE

    Will you sir? Commit the rascals.

DICK

    Commit with us! He were as good commit with his father,
    as commit with us.

FAUSTUS

    I do beseech your grace let them come in,
    They are good subject for a merriment.   50

DUKE

    Do as thou wilt Faustus, I give thee leave.

FAUSTUS

    I thank your grace.

Enter the CLOWN [ROBIN], DICK, CARTER, *and* HORSE-COURSER

                    Why, how now my good friends?
    'Faith, you are too outrageous, but come near,
    I have procured your pardons: welcome all.

ROBIN

    Nay sir, we will be welcome for our money, and we will   55
    pay for what we take: what ho! Give's half a dozen of beer
    here, and be hanged.

FAUSTUS

    Nay, hark you, can you tell me where you are?

CARTER

    Ay, marry can I, we are under heaven.

SERVANT

    Ay, but sir sauce-box, know you in what place?   60

HORSE-COURSER

    Ay, ay, the house is good enough to drink in. Zounds, fill
    us some beer, or we'll break all the barrels in the house, and
    dash out all your brains with your bottles.

FAUSTUS

    Be not so furious: come, you shall have beer.

---

46 *Commit* Take to prison; through frequent collocations such as 'commit
    adultery' the word came to have the sense of 'fornicate', which Dick
    assumes in the next line.

55ff The Clowns believe that, as they promised at the end of IV.vi, they
    have simply stepped into 'another room', whereas it would appear that
    Faustus, by his magic spells, has brought them unawares to the court
    of Vanholt.

My lord, beseech you give me leave awhile, 65
I'll gage my credit, 'twill content your grace.

DUKE

With all my heart, kind doctor, please thyself:
Our servants, and our court's at thy command.

FAUSTUS

I humbly thank your grace: then fetch some beer.

HORSE-COURSER

Ay, marry, there spake a doctor indeed, and 'faith I'll drink 70
a health to thy wooden leg for that word.

FAUSTUS

My wooden leg? What dost thou mean by that?

CARTER

Ha, ha, ha, dost thou hear him Dick? He has forgot his leg.

HORSE-COURSER

Ay, ay, he does not stand much upon that.

FAUSTUS

No 'faith, not much upon a wooden leg. 75

CARTER

Good Lord, that flesh and blood should be so frail with
your worship! Do not you remember a horse-courser you
sold a horse to?

FAUSTUS

Yes, I remember one I sold a horse.

CARTER

And do you remember you bid he should not ride into the 80
water?

FAUSTUS

Yes, I do very well remember that.

CARTER

And do you remember nothing of your leg?

FAUSTUS

No, in good sooth.

CARTER

Then I pray remember your curtsy. 85

FAUSTUS

I thank you sir.   [*He bows to the company*]

---

66 *gage* stake

73 ff The writer plays on the literal and metaphorical (=bow) uses of *leg*.
In line 74 the Horse-courser says, in effect, that Faustus does not
stand much upon ceremony.

85 *curtsy* (curtesie B) One of B's meanings is lost in modernizing the word
either as 'courtesy' or as 'curtsy'; the latter seems preferable since
it sustains the joke.

CARTER

'Tis not so much worth; I pray you tell me one thing.

FAUSTUS

What's that?

CARTER

Be both your legs bedfellows every night together?

FAUSTUS

Would'st thou make a colossus of me, that thou askest me　　90
such questions?

CARTER

No truly sir, I would make nothing of you, but I would fain
know that.

Enter HOSTESS *with drink*

FAUSTUS

Then I assure thee certainly they are.

CARTER

I thank you, I am fully satisfied.　　　　　　　　　　　95

FAUSTUS

But wherefore dost thou ask?

CARTER

For nothing sir–but methinks you should have a wooden
bedfellow of one of 'em.

HORSE-COURSER

Why, do you hear sir, did not I pull off one of your legs
when you were asleep?　　　　　　　　　　　　　　100

FAUSTUS

But I have it again now I am awake: look you here sir.

ALL

O horrible! Had the doctor three legs?

CARTER

Do you remember sir, how you cozened me and eat up my
load of—

　　　　　　　　　　　　　　　FAUSTUS *charms him dumb*

DICK

Do you remember how you made me wear an ape's—　　105

HORSE-COURSER

You whoreson conjuring scab, do you remember how you
cozened me with a ho—

---

87 *'Tis not so much worth* Faustus' bow is not worth much as an
　　indication of whether or not he has a wooden leg
90 *colossus* gigantic statue; the Colossus at Rhodes straddled the
　　entrance to the harbour; *cf. Julius Caesar*, I.ii, 135–6

ROBIN
  Ha' you forgotten me? You think to carry it away with your
  hey-pass and re-pass: do you remember the dog's fa—
                                              Exeunt CLOWNS

HOSTESS
  Who pays for the ale? Hear you maister doctor, now you   110
  have sent away my guests, I pray who shall pay me for my
  a—
                                              Exit HOSTESS

LADY
  My lord,
  We are much beholding to this learned man.

DUKE
  So are we, madam, which we will recompense   115
  With all the love and kindness that we may;
  His artful sport drives all sad thoughts away.
                                              Exeunt

Act V, Scene i

Thunder and lightning: Enter DEVILS *with covered dishes:*
MEPHOSTOPHILIS *leads them into* FAUSTUS' *study. Then
                      enter* WAGNER

WAGNER
  I think my master means to die shortly,
  For he hath given to me all his goods;
  And yet, methinks, if that death were near,
  He would not banquet, and carouse, and swill
  Amongst the students, as even now he doth,   5
  Who are at supper with such belly-cheer,
  As Wagner ne'er beheld in all his life.
  See where they come: belike the feast is ended.   *Exit*

109 *hey-pass and re-pass* abracadabra

1–8 At this point B gives Wagner a prose speech containing the gist of
   A's verse but adding:

     he hath made his will, and given me his wealth, his house, his
     goods, and store of golden plate; besides two thousand duckets
     ready coined.

   Most editors conflate the two, but it seems to me that a choice must
   be made; A's version, I think, is preferable, if only because by omitting
   mention of the will it avoids repetition at V.ii, 18*ff.*

Enter FAUSTUS, MEPHOSTOPHILIS, *and two or three* SCHOLARS

1 SCHOLAR
    Master Doctor Faustus, since our conference about fair
    ladies, which was the beautifullest in all the world, we have   10
    determined with ourselves, that Helen of Greece was the
    admirablest lady that ever lived: therefore, master doctor,
    if you will do us so much favour, as to let us see that peerless
    dame of Greece, we should think ourselves much beholding
    unto you.   15
FAUSTUS
    Gentlemen,
    For that I know your friendship is unfeigned,
    And Faustus' custom is not to deny
    The just requests of those that wish him well:
    You shall behold that peerless dame of Greece,   20
    No otherways for pomp and majesty,
    Than when Sir Paris crossed the seas with her,
    And brought the spoils to rich Dardania:
    Be silent then, for danger is in words.
        Music sound: MEPHOSTOPHILIS *brings in* HELEN; *she*
                                passeth over the stage
2 SCHOLAR
    Too simple is my wit to tell her praise,   25
    Whom all the world admires for majesty.
3 SCHOLAR
    No marvel though the angry Greeks pursued
    With ten years' war the rape of such a queen,
    Whose heavenly beauty passeth all compare.

23 *Dardania* Troy; in fact the city built by Dardanus on the Helles-
    pont, but the name is often transferred to Troy

13–14 *peerless dame of Greece* Here both texts anticipate Faustus at 1.20, and
    then both add 'whom all the world admires for majesty', thereby
    anticipating the Second Scholar's remark at 1.26. Greg, who detects
    revision in prompt-book at this point, suggests that the speech was
    written as part of this revision and copied by B from A. The revision
    must have been very careless. To my mind it seems more likely that
    the confusion is due to the A reporter.
24 s.d. *passeth over* It would appear that the character was instructed to
    move from one side of the yard, across the stage, and out at the other
    side of the yard, instead of entering by the stage doors (*cf.* Allardyce
    Nicoll, 'Passing Over the Stage', *Shakespeare Survey*, XII (1959),
    pp. 47–55).

1 SCHOLAR

   Since we have seen the pride of Nature's works,   30
   And only paragon of excellence,
   Let us depart, and for this glorious deed
   Happy and blest be Faustus evermore.

FAUSTUS

   Gentlemen farewell; the same I wish to you.

                           Exeunt SCHOLARS

Enter an OLD MAN

OLD MAN

   O gentle Faustus, leave this damned art,   35
   This magic, that will charm thy soul to hell,
   And quite bereave thee of salvation.
   Though thou hast now offended like a man,
   Do not persever in it like a devil;
   Yet, yet, thou hast an amiable soul,   40
   If sin by custom grow not into nature:
   Then, Faustus, will repentance come too late,
   Then thou art banished from the sight of heaven;
   No mortal can express the pains of hell.
   It may be this my exhortation   45
   Seems harsh, and all unpleasant; let it not,
   For, gentle son, I speak it not in wrath,
   Or envy of thee, but in tender love,

35–51 A's version of the Old Man's speech is printed in the Appendix (p. 100)
39 *persever* Accented on the second syllable
40–41 Your soul is still capable of being loved, so long as sin does not become habitual and thus part of your nature

---

25–33 In the B Text the Scholars' comments are as follows:

    2 SCHOLAR
       Was this fair Helen, whose admired worth
       Made Greece with ten years' war afflict poor Troy?
    3 SCHOLAR
       Too simple is my wit to tell her worth,
       Whom all the world admires for majesty.
    1 SCHOLAR
       Now we have seen the pride of Nature's work
       We'll take our leaves, and for this blessed sight,
       Happy and blest be Faustus evermore.

Greg attributes the superiority of A's version to Marlowe's having revised the lines. I doubt this; the multiple repetitions and other weaknesses sound more like very bad reporting–although I confess I cannot see how this fits in with any theory about the nature of the B text.

And pity of thy future misery;
And so have hope, that this my kind rebuke,   50
Checking thy body, may amend thy soul.

FAUSTUS

Where art thou Faustus, wretch, what hast thou done?
Damned art thou Faustus, damned; despair and die!

              MEPHOSTOPHILIS *gives him a dagger*

Hell claims his right, and with a roaring voice
Says 'Faustus come, thine hour is almost come',   55
And Faustus now will come to do thee right.

              [FAUSTUS *goes to use the dagger*]

OLD MAN

O stay, good Faustus, stay thy desperate steps!
I see an angel hover o'er thy head,
And with a vial full of precious grace,
Offers to pour the same into thy soul;   60
Then call for mercy, and avoid despair.

FAUSTUS

O friend, I feel
Thy words to comfort my distressed soul:
Leave me awhile, to ponder on my sins.

OLD MAN

Faustus I leave thee, but with grief of heart,   65
Fearing the enemy of thy hapless soul.   *Exit*

FAUSTUS

Accursed Faustus, where is mercy now?
I do repent, and yet I do despair;
Hell strives with grace for conquest in my breast:
What shall I do to shun the snares of death?   70

MEPHOSTOPHILIS

Thou traitor Faustus, I arrest thy soul
For disobedience to my sovereign lord.
Revolt, or I'll in piecemeal tear thy flesh.

FAUSTUS

I do repent I e'er offended him;
Sweet Mephostophilis, entreat thy lord   75
To pardon my unjust presumption,
And with my blood again I will confirm
The former vow I made to Lucifer.

53 A (*not in* B)
66 *enemy* B (ruin A);
   hapless B (hopeless A)
67 *where is mercy now* A (wretch, what hast thou done B)
73 *Revolt* Turn again to your allegiance
74 B (*not in* A)

MEPHOSTOPHILIS

    Do it then quickly with unfeigned heart,
    Lest greater dangers do attend thy drift.   80

FAUSTUS

    Torment, sweet friend, that base and crooked age,
    That durst dissuade me from thy Lucifer,
    With greatest torment that our hell affords.

MEPHOSTOPHILIS

    His faith is great, I cannot touch his soul;
    But what I may afflict his body with,   85
    I will attempt, which is but little worth.

FAUSTUS

    One thing, good servant, let me crave of thee,
    To glut the longing of my heart's desire,
    That I may have unto my paramour,
    That heavenly Helen, which I saw of late,   90
    Whose sweet embracings may extinguish clear
    Those thoughts that do dissuade me from my vow,
    And keep mine oath I made to Lucifer.

MEPHOSTOPHILIS

    This, or what else my Faustus shall desire,
    Shall be performed in twinkling of an eye.   95

Enter HELEN *again, passing over between two* CUPIDS

FAUSTUS

    Was this the face that launched a thousand ships,
    And burnt the topless towers of Ilium?
    Sweet Helen, make me immortal with a kiss:
    Her lips suck forth my soul, see where it flies!

79 *quickly* A (Faustus B)
80 *drift* drifting; also purpose
81 *base and crooked age* A (base and aged man B)
91 *embracings* A (embraces B)
93 *mine oath* A (my vow B)
97 *Ilium* Troy

96–104 In these lines Marlowe is repeating his own memorable phrases:
        Helen, whose beauty summoned Greece to arms,
        And drew a thousand ships to Tenedos.
                2 *Tamburlaine*, II.iv, 87–8
        And he'll make me immortal with a kiss.
                Dido, IV.iv, 123
        So thou wouldst prove as true as Paris did,
        Would, as fair Troy was, Carthage might be sacked,
        And I be called a second Helena.
                Dido, V.i, 146–8

Come Helen, come, give me my soul again.   100
Here will I dwell, for heaven is in these lips,
And all is dross that is not Helena.

Enter OLD MAN

I will be Paris, and for love of thee,
Instead of Troy shall Wittenberg be sacked;
And I will combat with weak Menelaus,   105
And wear thy colours on my plumed crest;
Yea, I will wound Achilles in the heel,
And then return to Helen for a kiss.
O, thou art fairer than the evening's air,
Clad in the beauty of a thousand stars: 110
Brighter art thou than flaming Jupiter,
When he appeared to hapless Semele;
More lovely than the monarch of the sky
In wanton Arethusa's azured arms;
And none but thou shalt be my paramour.   115
                    Exeunt [FAUSTUS *and* HELEN]

OLD MAN
Accursed Faustus, miserable man,
That from thy soul exclud'st the grace of heaven,
And fliest the throne of His tribunal seat!

Enter the DEVILS

Satan begins to sift me with his pride,
As in this furnace God shall try my faith: 120
My faith, vile hell, shall triumph over thee!
Ambitious fiends, see how the heavens smiles
At your repulse, and laughs your state to scorn!
Hence hell, for hence I fly unto my God.   *Exeunt*

---

102 s.d. This direction, and the Old Man's final speech (116–24) are
    missing from B
111–12 The sight of Jupiter in all his divine splendour was too much for
    mortal eyes, and Semele was consumed by the fire of his brightness.
113–14 No myth has been traced linking the sun-god with Arethusa; the
    nymph was changed into a fountain, and perhaps Marlowe is referring
    to the reflection of the sun in blue waters.

Act V, Scene ii

Thunder. Enter LUCIFER, BELZEBUB, *and* MEPHOSTOPHILIS

LUCIFER

Thus from infernal Dis do we ascend
To view the subjects of our monarchy,
Those souls which sin seals the black sons of hell,
'Mong which as chief, Faustus, we come to thee,
Bringing with us lasting damnation,　　　　　　　　　　5
To wait upon thy soul; the time is come
Which makes it forfeit.

MEPHOSTOPHILIS　　　　　　　And this gloomy night,
Here in this room will wretched Faustus be.

BELZEBUB

And here we'll stay,
To mark him how he doth demean himself.　　　　　　10

MEPHOSTOPHILIS

How should he, but in desperate lunacy?
Fond worldling, now his heart-blood dries with grief,
His conscience kills it, and his labouring brain,
Begets a world of idle fantasies,
To overreach the devil; but all in vain:　　　　　　　15
His store of pleasures must be sauced with pain.
He and his servant Wagner are at hand,
Both come from drawing Faustus' latest will.
See where they come.

Enter FAUSTUS *and* WAGNER

FAUSTUS

Say Wagner, thou hast perused my will,　　　　　　20
How dost thou like it?

WAGNER　　　　　　　　　Sir, so wondrous well,
As in all humble duty, I do yield
My life and lasting service for your love.

FAUSTUS

Gramercies Wagner.　　　　　　　　　[*Exit* WAGNER]

---

1 *Dis* The Underworld; an alternative name for Pluto and extended
to his kingdom

Act V, Scene ii. Textually the most vexed portion of the play. The infernal
conclave (ll. 1–23), the interview with Mephostophilis (11.85–96), and
the visions of heaven and hell (11.97–130) are found only in the B Text.
If the first two are indeed Marlowe's, the play takes on a quite different
nature from that indicated by the first and last soliloquies. See
Introduction, p. xviii.

Enter the SCHOLARS

　　　　Welcome gentlemen.

1 SCHOLAR

Now worthy Faustus, methinks your looks are changed.　　25

FAUSTUS

Ah, gentlemen!

2 SCHOLAR

What ails Faustus?

FAUSTUS

Ah my sweet chamber-fellow, had I lived with thee, then
had I lived still, but now must die eternally. Look sirs,
comes he not, comes he not?　　30

1 SCHOLAR

O my dear Faustus, what imports this fear?

2 SCHOLAR

Is all our pleasure turned to melancholy?

3 SCHOLAR

He is not well with being over-solitary.

2 SCHOLAR

If it be so, we'll have physicians, and Faustus shall be cured.

3 SCHOLAR

'Tis but a surfeit sir, fear nothing.　　35

FAUSTUS

A surfeit of deadly sin, that hath damned both body and
soul.

2 SCHOLAR

Yet Faustus, look up to heaven, and remember God's mercy
is infinite.

FAUSTUS

But Faustus' offence can ne'er be pardoned. The serpent　　40
that tempted Eve may be saved, but not Faustus. Ah gentlemen, hear with patience, and tremble not at my speeches;
though my heart pants and quivers to remember that I
have been a student here these thirty years—O would I had
never seen Wittenberg, never read book—and what wonders　　45
I have done, all Germany can witness, yea, all the world—
for which Faustus hath lost both Germany and the world
—yea, heaven itself—heaven, the seat of God, the throne of
the blessed, the kingdom of joy; and must remain in hell

38-39 *God's mercy is infinite* ed. (God's mercies are infinite A; mercy is
infinite B) B's reading, with the addition of A's *God's* (omitted, perhaps,
by the censoring editor) is the more appropriate; Faustus is being
reminded that God's power of forgiveness is boundless, not that his
blessings are without number

for ever. Hell, ah hell, for ever! Sweet friends, what shall   50
become of Faustus, being in hell for ever?

2 SCHOLAR

Yet Faustus, call on God.

FAUSTUS

On God, whom Faustus hath abjured? On God, whom
Faustus hath blasphemed? Ah my God—I would weep,
but the devil draws in my tears. Gush forth blood instead   55
of tears, yea, life and soul. O, he stays my tongue! I would
lift up my hands, but see, they hold 'em, they hold 'em.

ALL

Who Faustus?

FAUSTUS

Why, Lucifer and Mephostophilis: ah gentlemen, I gave
them my soul for my cunning.   60

ALL

God forbid!

FAUSTUS

God forbade it indeed, but Faustus hath done it. For the
vain pleasure of four and twenty years hath Faustus lost
eternal joy and felicity. I writ them a bill with mine own
blood: the date is expired, this is the time, and he will fetch   65
me.

1 SCHOLAR

Why did not Faustus tell us of this before, that divines
might have prayed for thee?

FAUSTUS

Oft have I thought to have done so, but the devil threatened
to tear me in pieces if I named God, to fetch me body and   70
soul if I once gave ear to divinity; and now 'tis too late.
Gentlemen, away: lest you perish with me.

2 SCHOLAR

O what may we do to save Faustus?

FAUSTUS

Talk not of me, but save yourselves and depart.

3 SCHOLAR

God will strengthen me. I will stay with Faustus.   75

1 SCHOLAR

Tempt not God, sweet friend, but let us into the next room,
and there pray for him.

54–5 'No not so much as their eyes are able to shed teares (thretten and
torture them as ye please) while first they repent (God not permitting
them to dissemble their obstinacie in so horrible a crime)'. *Daemonologie*,
p. 81.

FAUSTUS

Ay, pray for me, pray for me; and what noise soever you
hear, come not unto me, for nothing can rescue me.

2 SCHOLAR

Pray thou, and we will pray, that God may have mercy upon   80
thee.

FAUSTUS

Gentlemen, farewell. If I live till morning, I'll visit you:
if not, Faustus is gone to hell.

ALL

Faustus, farewell.   *Exeunt* SCHOLARS

MEPHOSTOPHILIS

Ay Faustus, now thou hast no hope of heaven,   85
Therefore despair, think only upon hell;
For that must be thy mansion, there to dwell.

FAUSTUS

O thou bewitching fiend, 'twas thy temptation,
Hath robbed me of eternal happiness.

MEPHOSTOPHILIS

I do confess it Faustus, and rejoice: 90
'Twas I that, when thou wert i'the way to heaven,
Damned up thy passage; when thou took'st the book,
To view the Scriptures, then I turned the leaves
And led thine eye.
What, weep'st thou? 'Tis too late, despair, farewell: 95
Fools that will laugh on earth, must weep in hell.   *Exit*

Enter the GOOD ANGEL, *and the* BAD ANGEL *at several doors*

GOOD ANGEL

O Faustus, if thou hadst given ear to me,
Innumerable joys had followed thee.
But thou didst love the world.

BAD ANGEL   Gave ear to me,
And now must taste hell's pains perpetually.   100

GOOD ANGEL

O what will all thy riches, pleasures, pomps,
Avail thee now?

BAD ANGEL   Nothing but vex thee more,
To want in hell, that had on earth such store.
                 Music while the throne descends

GOOD ANGEL

O thou hast lost celestial happiness,
Pleasures unspeakable, bliss without end.   105
Hadst thou affected sweet divinity,
Hell, or the devil, had had no power on thee.

Hadst thou kept on that way, Faustus, behold,
In what resplendent glory thou hadst sat
In yonder throne, like those bright shining saints,   110
And triumphed over hell; that hast thou lost,
And now, poor soul, must thy good angel leave thee:
The jaws of hell are open to receive thee.

Exit [the throne ascends]
Hell is discovered

BAD ANGEL
Now Faustus, let thine eyes with horror stare
Into that vast perpetual torture-house.   115
There are the furies tossing damned souls
On burning forks; there bodies boil in lead;
There are live quarters broiling on the coals,
That ne'er can die; this ever-burning chair,
Is for o'er-tortured souls to rest them in;   120
These, that are fed with sops of flaming fire,
Were gluttons, and loved only delicates,
And laughed to see the poor starve at their gates:
But yet all these are nothing: thou shalt see
Ten thousand tortures that more horrid be.   125
FAUSTUS
O, I have seen enough to torture me.
BAD ANGEL
Nay, thou must feel them, taste the smart of all:
He that loves pleasure, must for pleasure fall.
And so I leave thee Faustus, till anon,
Then wilt thou tumble in confusion.   *Exit*   130

The clock strikes eleven

FAUSTUS
Ah Faustus,
Now hast thou but one bare hour to live,
And then thou must be damned perpetually.
Stand still, you ever-moving spheres of heaven,
That time may cease, and midnight never come.   135
Fair nature's eye, rise, rise again and make
Perpetual day; or let this hour be but
A year, a month, a week, a natural day,

134–7 *Cf. Edward II*, V.i, 64–8:
    Continue ever, thou celestial sun;
    Let never silent night possess this clime:
    Stand still you watches of the element;
    All times and seasons, rest you at a stay,
    That Edward may be still fair England's king.

That Faustus may repent, and save his soul.
O lente, lente currite noctis equi!   140
The stars move still, time runs, the clock will strike,
The devil will come, and Faustus must be damned.
O I'll leap up to my God! Who pulls me down?
See, see where Christ's blood streams in the firmament!
One drop would save my soul, half a drop. Ah my Christ— 145
Rend not my heart for naming of my Christ;
Yet will I call on him: O spare me Lucifer!
Where is it now? 'Tis gone, and see where God
Stretcheth out his arm, and bends his ireful brows:
Mountains and hills, come, come, and fall on me,   150
And hide me from the heavy wrath of God.
No, no!
Then will I headlong run into the earth:
Earth, gape! O no, it will not harbour me.
You stars that reigned at my nativity,   155
Whose influence hath allotted death and hell,
Now draw up Faustus like a foggy mist
Into the entrails of yon labouring cloud,
That when you vomit forth into the air,
My limbs may issue from your smoky mouths,   160
So that my soul may but ascend to heaven.

                                        The watch strikes

Ah, half the hour is past; 'twill all be past anon!
O God,

140 Gallop slowly, slowly, you horses of the night
143 *my God* A (heaven B)
144 A (*not in* B)
148 *it* the vision of God; the momentary yielding to terror and the
      devil banishes even this remote vision of mercy
148–9 *see where . . . brows* A (see a threatening arm, an angry brow B)
151 *God* A (heaven B)

---

140 The final and most famous irony of the play. The line is from Ovid's
      Amores, I.xiii, 40, where the poet longs for never-ending night in the
      arms of his mistress.
150–51 'And they shall say to the mountains, Cover us; and to the hills,
      Fall on us', Hosea, x,8 (See also Revelations, vi,16 and Luke, xxiii,3);
      Looking Glass for London has the same idea:
          Hell gapes for me, heaven will not hold my soule,
          You mountaines shroude me from the God of truth . . .
          Cover me hills, and shroude me from the Lord. 11.2054–5,9.
155–61 Faustus prays the stars, whose positions at his birth ordained this
      fate, to suck him up into a cloud as a fog or mist is drawn up, and then
      in a storm expel his body in order that his soul may be saved. Instead of
      So that at 1.61 B reads 'But let'; Greg suggests that the B editor 'felt
      that A's text smacked too much of a bargain with heaven'.

If thou wilt not have mercy on my soul,
Yet for Christ's sake, whose blood hath ransomed me, 165
Impose some end to my incessant pain:
Let Faustus live in hell a thousand years,
A hundred thousand, and at last be saved.
O, no end is limited to damned souls!
Why wert thou not a creature wanting soul? 170
Or why is this immortal that thou hast?
Ah, Pythagoras' *metempsychosis*–were that true,
This soul should fly from me, and I be changed
Unto some brutish beast.
All beasts are happy, for when they die, 175
Their souls are soon dissolved in elements;
But mine must live still to be plagued in hell.
Cursed be the parents that engendered me!
No Faustus, curse thyself, curse Lucifer,
That hath deprived thee of the joys of heaven. 180
       The clock striketh twelve
It strikes, it strikes! Now body turn to air,
Or Lucifer will bear thee quick to hell.
       Thunder and lightning
O soul, be changed into little water drops,
And fall into the ocean, ne'er be found.
      Enter the DEVILS

My God, my God! Look not so fierce on me! 185
Adders, and serpents, let me breathe awhile!
Ugly hell gape not! Come not Lucifer;
I'll burn my books–ah Mephostophilis! *Exeunt with him*

Act V, Scene iii

Enter the SCHOLARS

1 SCHOLAR
 Come gentlemen, let us go visit Faustus,
 For such a dreadful night was never seen

163–4 *O God . . . soul* A (O, if my soul must suffer for my sin B)
182 *quick* living
183 little A (small B)
V.iii. This scene is not in the A Text

---

172 *Pythagoras' metempsychosis* The theory of the transmigration of souls,
 attributed to Pythagoras, whereby the human soul at the death of the
 body took on some other form of life.
188 *I'll burn my books* All magicians who renounced their art made a solemn
 act of disposing of their books of magic; *cf. The Tempest*, V.i, 56–7.

Since first the world's creation did begin;
Such fearful shrieks, and cries were never heard.
Pray heaven the doctor have escaped the danger.   5

2 SCHOLAR

O help us heaven! See, here are Faustus' limbs,
All torn asunder by the hand of death.

3 SCHOLAR

The devils whom Faustus served have torn him thus:
For 'twixt the hours of twelve and one, methought
I heard him shriek and call aloud for help: 10
At which self time the house seemed all on fire,
With dreadful horror of these damned fiends.

2 SCHOLAR

Well Gentlemen, though Faustus' end be such
As every Christian heart laments to think on;
Yet for he was a scholar, once admired   15
For wondrous knowledge in our German schools,
We'll give his mangled limbs due burial,
And all the students clothed in mourning black,
Shall wait upon his heavy funeral.   *Exeunt*

EPILOGUE

Enter CHORUS

CHORUS

Cut is the branch that might have grown full straight,
And burned is Apollo's laurel bough,
That sometime grew within this learned man.
Faustus is gone: regard his hellish fall,
Whose fiendful fortune may exhort the wise   5
Only to wonder at unlawful things:
Whose deepness doth entice such forward wits,
To practise more than heavenly power permits.

                                                      [*Exit*]

Terminat hora diem, terminat author opus

FINIS

16 *schools* universities
19 *heavy* sorrowful

Terminat . . . opus The hour ends the day, the author ends his work.
The origin is unknown, and it seems likely that the line was appended
to the play by the printer and not by Marlowe.

APPENDIX

Major variants in the A Text

Act II, Scene iii

Enter ROBIN *the Ostler with a book in his hand*

ROBIN
O this is admirable! Here I ha' stolen one of Doctor Faustus'
conjuring books and, 'faith, I mean to search some circles
for my own use. Now will I make all the maidens in our
parish dance at my pleasure stark naked before me, and so
by that means I shall see more than e'er I felt or saw yet.   5

Enter RALPH, *calling* ROBIN

RALPH
Robin, prithee come away. There's a gentleman tarries to
have his horse, and he would have his things rubbed and
made clean; he keeps such a chafing with my mistress about
it, and she has sent me to look thee out. Prithee come away.
ROBIN
Keep out, keep out, or else you are blown up, you are dis-   10
membered, Ralph; keep out, for I am about a roaring piece
of work.
RALPH
Come, what dost thou with that same book? Thou canst not
read.
ROBIN
Yes, my master and mistress shall find that I can read, he   15
for his forehead, she for her private study; she's born to
bear with me, or else my art fails.
RALPH
Why Robin, what book is that?
ROBIN
What book? Why, the most intolerable book for conjuring
that e'er was invented by any brimstone devil.   20
RALPH
Canst thou conjure with it?

2 *circles* magicians' circles; but the sexual overtones are obvious
11 *roaring* wild and dangerous
19 *intolerable* Robin probably means incomparable

90

ROBIN

I can do all these things easily with it: first, I can make thee
drunk with hippocras at any tavern in Europe for nothing
–that's one of my conjuring works.

RALPH

Our master parson says that's nothing.   25

ROBIN

True Ralph, and more Ralph, if thou hast any mind to
Nan Spit our kitchen maid, then turn her and wind her
to thy own use, as often as thou wilt, and at midnight.

RALPH

O brave, Robin, shall I have Nan Spit, and to mine own use?
On that condition I'll feed thy devil with horse-bread as   30
long as he lives, of free cost.

ROBIN

No more, sweet Ralph; let's go and make clean our boots
which lie foul upon our hands, and then to our conjuring,
in the devil's name.   *Exeunt*

Act III, Scene iii

Enter ROBIN *and* RALPH *with a silver goblet*

ROBIN

Come Ralph, did not I tell thee we were made for ever by
this Doctor Faustus' book? *Ecce signum*, here's a simple
purchase for horse-keepers; our horses shall eat no hay
as long as this lasts.

RALPH

But Robin, here comes the vintner.   5

ROBIN

Hush, I'll gull him supernaturally. Drawer, I hope all is
paid. God be with you. Come, Ralph.

VINTNER

Soft, sir, a word with you. I must yet have a goblet paid
from you ere you go.

ROBIN

I, a goblet, Ralph! I, a goblet! I scorn you; and you are   10
but a etc. I, a goblet! Search me.

2 *Ecce signum* Behold the proof; a catchword fairly frequent among
the Clowns; *cf. I Henry IV*, II.iv, 149
simple purchase piece of clear profit
6 *gull* trick
11 *etc.* This probably indicated that the Clown was to fill in with any
comic terms of abuse that came to his mind

VINTNER

I mean so, sir, with your favour.   [*Searches him*]

ROBIN

How say you now?

VINTNER

I must say somewhat to your fellow. You sir!

RALPH

Me, sir! Me, sir! Search your fill.   [VINTNER *searches him*]   15
Now sir, you may be ashamed to burden honest men with
a matter of truth.

VINTNER

Well, t'one of you hath this goblet about you.

ROBIN

You lie, drawer, 'tis afore me. Sirra, you, I'll teach ye to
impeach honest men. Stand by. I'll scour you for a goblet.   20
Stand aside, you had best. I charge you in the name of
Belzebub – look to the goblet Ralph.

VINTNER

What mean you sirra?

ROBIN

I'll tell you what I mean.   *He reads*
Sanctobulorum Periphrasticon – nay, I'll tickle you, vintner –   25
look to the goblet Ralph – *Polypragmos, Belseborams framanto
pacostiphos tostu Mephostophilis etc.*

    Enter MEPHOSTOPHILIS: *sets squibs at their backs:
                they run about*

VINTNER

O nomine Domine, what meanest thou Robin? thou hast no
goblet.

RALPH

Peccatum peccatorum, here's thy goblet, good Vintner.   30

ROBIN

Misericordia pro nobis, what shall I do? Good devil, forgive
me now, and I'll never rob thy library more.

            Enter to them MEPHOSTOPHILIS

MEPHOSTOPHILIS

Vanish villains, th'one like an ape, another like a bear, the
third an ass, for doing this enterprise.
Monarch of hell, under whose black survey   35

20 *scour you* settle you, polish you off

28–32 The dog-Latin marks the Clowns' attempts to protect themselves
    from the devil; 'Nominus patrus, I bless me from thee' *Looking Glass
    for London*, line 1698.
33–49 These lines must constitute an alternative ending to the scene.

Great potentates do kneel with awful fear,
Upon whose altars thousand souls do lie,
How am I vexed with these villains' charms!
From Constantinople am I hither come,
Only for pleasure of these damned slaves   40
ROBIN
How, from Constantinople? You have had a great journey.
Will you take sixpence in your purse to pay for your supper
and be gone?
MEPHOSTOPHILIS
Well, villains, for your presumption, I transform thee into
an ape, and thee into a dog, and so be gone.   *Exit*   45
ROBIN
How, into an ape? That's brave! I'll have fine sport with
the boys, I'll get nuts and apples enow.
RALPH
And I must be a dog.
ROBIN
I'faith, thy head will never be out of the potage pot.
                                                    Exeunt

Act IV, Scene ii

Enter EMPEROR, FAUSTUS, *and a* KNIGHT *with* ATTENDANTS

EMPEROR
Master Doctor Faustus, I have heard strange report of thy
knowledge in the black art, how that none in my empire,
nor in the whole world can compare with thee for the rare
effects of magic. They say thou hast a familiar spirit by
whom thou canst accomplish what thou list. This therefore   5
is my request: that thou let me see some proof of thy skill,
that mine eyes may be witnesses to confirm what mine ears
have heard reported; and here I swear to thee, by the honour
of mine imperial crown, that whatever thou dost, thou shalt
be no ways prejudiced or endamaged.   10
KNIGHT
I'faith, he looks much like a conjuror.   *Aside*
FAUSTUS
My gracious sovereign, though I must confess myself far
inferior to the report men have published and nothing
answerable to the honour of your imperial Majesty, yet for

13–14 *nothing answerable to* in no way worthy of

that love and duty binds me thereunto, I am content to do   15
whatsoever your majesty shall command me.

EMPEROR

Then Doctor Faustus, mark what I shall say.
As I was sometime solitary set
Within my closet, sundry thoughts arose
About the honour of mine ancestors;   20
How they had won by prowess such exploits,
Got such riches, subdued so many kingdoms,
As we that do succeed, or they that shall
Hereafter possess our throne, shall,
I fear me, never attain to that degree   25
Of high renown and great authority;
Amongst which kings is Alexander the Great,
Chief spectacle of the world's pre-eminence,
The bright shining of whose glorious acts
Lightens the world with his reflecting beams;   30
As when I hear but motion made of him,
It grieves my soul I never saw the man.
If, therefore, thou, by cunning of thine art,
Canst raise this man from hollow vaults below,
Where lies entombed this famous conqueror,   35
And bring with him his beauteous paramour,
Both in their right shapes, gesture and attire
They used to wear during their time of life,
Thou shalt both satisfy my just desire,
And give me cause to praise thee whilst I live.   40

FAUSTUS

My gracious lord, I am ready to accomplish your request
so far forth as by art and power of my spirit I am able to
perform.

KNIGHT

I'faith, that's just nothing at all.   *Aside*

FAUSTUS

But if it like your Grace, it is not in my ability to present   45
before your eyes the true substantial bodies of those two
deceased princes, which long since are consumed to dust.

KNIGHT

Ay, marry master doctor, now there's a sign of grace in you,
when you will confess the truth.   *Aside*

FAUSTUS

But such spirits as can lively resemble Alexander and his   50

28 *pre-eminence* pre-eminent men; *cf.* the two uses of 'nobility'
31 *motion* mention
37 *gesture* manner

paramour shall appear before your Grace, in that manner
that they best lived in, in their most flourishing estate; which
I doubt not shall sufficiently content your imperial Majesty.

EMPEROR

Go to, master doctor, let me see them presently.

KNIGHT

Do you hear, master doctor? You bring Alexander and his   55
paramour before the Emperor.

FAUSTUS

How then sir?

KNIGIIT

I'faith, that's as true as Diana turned me to a stag.

FAUSTUS

No sir, but when Actaeon died, he left the horns for you.
Mephostophilis, begone!   60

Exit MEPHOSTOPHILIS

KNIGHT

Nay, and you go to conjuring, I'll be gone.

Exit KNIGHT

FAUSTUS

I'll meet with you anon for interrupting me so–Here they
are, my gracious lord.

Enter MEPHOSTOPHILIS *with* ALEXANDER *and his* PARAMOUR

EMPEROR

Master doctor, I heard this lady, while she lived, had a wart
or mole in her neck. How shall I know whether it be so or no?   65

FAUSTUS

Your Highness may boldly go and see.

EMPEROR

Sure these are no spirits but the true substantial bodies of
those two deceased princes.

Exit ALEXANDER [*and* PARAMOUR]

FAUSTUS

Will't please your Highness now to send for the knight that
was so pleasant with me here of late?   70

EMPEROR

One of you call him forth.

Enter the KNIGHT *with a pair of horns on his head*

EMPEROR

How now sir knight? Why, I had thought thou hadst been

58 *Diana . . . stag* (see note on IV.ii, 51)
62 *meet with you anon* get even with you soon
70 *pleasant* facetious

a bachelor, but now I see thou hast wife, that not only gives
thee horns, but makes thee wear them. Feel on thy head.

KNIGHT

Thou damned wretch and execrable dog,   75
Bred in the concave of some monstrous rock!
How dar'st thou thus abuse a gentleman?
Villain, I say, undo what thou hast done.

FAUSTUS

O, not so fast sir, there's no haste but good. Are you
remembered how you crossed me in my conference with   80
the Emperor? I think I have met with you for it.

EMPEROR

Good master doctor, at my entreaty release him; he hath
done penance sufficient.

FAUSTUS

My gracious lord, not so much for the injury he offered me
here in your presence, as to delight you with some mirth,   85
hath Faustus worthily requited this injurious knight; which
being all I desire, I am content to release him of his horns:
and, sir knight, hereafter speak well of scholars. Mephostophilis, transform him straight. Now my good lord, having
done my duty, I humbly take my leave.   90

EMPEROR

Farewell master doctor; yet ere you go, expect from me a
bounteous reward.

Exit EMPEROR [KNIGHT *and* ATTENDANTS]

Act IV, Scene v

FAUSTUS

Now, Mephostophilis, the restless course
That time doth run with calm and silent foot,
Shortening my days and thread of vital life,
Calls for the payment of my latest years.
Therefore sweet Mephostophilis, let us   5
Make haste to Wittenberg.

MEPHOSTOPHILIS   What, will you go
On horseback, or on foot?

---

76 *concave* hollow; the same expression is in 2 *Tamburlaine*, II.ii, 89
79 *no haste but good* Proverb (Tilley, H 199)
84 *injury* insult
IV.v. At the end of the court scene Faustus and Mephostophilis
apparently remain on stage for the scene that follows

FAUSTUS   Nay, till I am past
This fair and pleasant green, I'll walk on foot.

Enter a HORSE-COURSER

HORSE-COURSER
I have been all this day seeking one maister Fustian. Mass,
see where he is! God save you, maister doctor.   10
FAUSTUS
What, horse-courser, you are well met.
HORSE-COURSER
Do you hear sir, I have brought you forty dollars for your
horse.
FAUSTUS
I cannot sell him so. If thou likest him for fifty, take him.
HORSE-COURSER
Alas, sir, I have no more. [*To* MEPHOSTOPHILIS] I pray you   15
speak for me.
MEPHOSTOPHILIS
I pray you, let him have him; he is an honest fellow and he
has a great charge, neither wife nor child.
FAUSTUS
Well, come, give me your money; my boy will deliver him
to you. But I must tell you one thing before you have him: 20
ride him not into the water at any hand.
HORSE-COURSER
Why, sir, will he not drink of all waters?
FAUSTUS
O yes, he will drink of all waters, but ride him not into the
water; ride him over hedge or ditch or where thou wilt, but
not into the water.   25
HORSE-COURSER
Well, sir. Now am I a made man for ever. I'll not leave my
horse for forty: if he had but the quality of hey-ding-
ding, hey-ding-ding, I'd make a brave living on him; he has
a buttock as slick as an eel. Well, God b'wi'ye, sir, your boy
will deliver him me. But hark ye sir, if my horse be sick, or   30
ill at ease, if I bring his water to you, you'll tell me what is?

---

21 *at any hand* on any account
22 *drink of all waters* (see note on IV.v, 13–14)
27 *for forty* for anything; forty is often used to indicate a large and
    imprecise number; *cf. Coriolanus*, III.i, 242
27–8 *the quality of hey-ding-ding* 'the Horse-courser must mean
    something by this. I suspect he means a complete horse, not a
    gelding' (Greg)

FAUSTUS

Away you villain! What, dost think I am a horse-doctor?

Exit HORSE-COURSER

What art thou, Faustus, but a man condemned to die?
Thy fatal time doth draw to final end;
Despair doth drive distrust unto my thoughts.   35
Confound these passions with a quiet sleep:
Tush, Christ did call the thief upon the cross;
Then rest thee, Faustus, quiet in conceit.

Sleep in his chair

Enter HORSE-COURSER *all wet, crying*

HORSE-COURSER

Alas, alas! Doctor Fustian, quotha? Mass, Doctor Lopus
was never such a doctor. Has given me a purgation, has   40
purged me of forty dollars; I shall never see them more. But
yet, like an ass as I was, I would not be ruled by him, for he
bade me I should ride him into no water. Now I, thinking
my horse had had some rare quality that he would not have
had me known of, I, like a venturous youth, rid him into the   45
deep pond at the town's end. I was no sooner in the middle
of the pond, but my horse vanished away, and I sat upon a
bottle of hay, never so near drowning in my life. But I'll
seek out my doctor, and have my forty dollars again, or I'll
make it the dearest horse. O, yonder is his snipper-snapper.   50
Do you hear? You, hey-pass, where's your maister?

MEPHOSTOPHILIS

Why sir, what would you? You cannot speak with him.

HORSE-COURSER

But I will speak with him.

MEPHOSTOPHILIS

Why, he's fast asleep. Come some other time.

HORSE-COURSER

I'll speak with him now, or I'll break his glass-windows   55
about his ears.

MEPHOSTOPHILIS

I tell thee he has not slept this eight nights.

---

50 *snipper-snapper* conceited young fellow
51 *hey-pass* mumbo-jumbo
55 *glass-windows* spectacles

---

39 *Doctor Lopus* Dr. Lopez, personal physician to Elizabeth, was executed
in 1594 for his supposed part in a plot to poison the Queen. This is
the most obvious instance of an actor's interpolation – Marlowe cannot
possibly have known about the Lopez scandal.

HORSE-COURSER

    And he have not slept this eight weeks I'll speak with him.

MEPHOSTOPHILIS

    See where he is fast asleep.

HORSE-COURSER

    Ay, this is he. God save ye, maister doctor. Maister doctor,   60
    maister Doctor Fustian! Forty dollars, forty dollars for a
    bottle of hay!

MEPHOSTOPHILIS

    Why, thou seest he hears thee not.

HORSE-COURSER

    So, ho, ho: so, ho, ho.

                              Holloa in his ear

    No, will you not wake? I'll make you wake ere I go.   65
                  Pull him by the leg, and pull it away

    Alas, I am undone! What shall I do?

FAUSTUS

    O my leg, my leg! Help Mephostophilis! Call the officers!
    My leg, my leg!

MEPHOSTOPHILIS

    Come, villain, to the constable.

HORSE-COURSER

    O Lord, sir, let me go, and I'll give you forty dollars more.   70

MEPHOSTOPHILIS

    Where be they?

HORSE-COURSER

    I have none about me. Come to my hostry and I'll give
    them you.

MEPHOSTOPHILIS

    Be gone quickly.   HORSE-COURSER *runs away*

FAUSTUS

    What, is he gone? Farewell he! Faustus has his leg again,   75
    and the horse-courser, I take it, a bottle of hay for his
    labour. Well, this trick shall cost him forty dollars more.

                 Enter WAGNER

How now, Wagner, what's the news with thee?

WAGNER

    Sir, the Duke of Vanholt doth earnestly entreat your
    company.   80

FAUSTUS

    The Duke of Vanholt! An honourable gentleman to whom

---

64 *So, ho, ho,* huntsman's cry to direct hounds to the hare

I must be no niggard of my cunning. Come Mephostophilis,
let's away to him.   *Exeunt*

Act V, Scene i, 35–51

The Old Man's speech.

OLD MAN

Ah, Doctor Faustus, that I might prevail
To guide thy steps unto the way of life,
By which sweet path thou may'st attain the goal
That shall conduct thee to celestial rest.
Break heart, drop blood, and mingle it with tears,   5
Tears falling from repentant heaviness
Of thy most vile and loathsome filthiness,
The stench whereof corrupts the inward soul
With such flagitious crimes of heinous sins,
As no commiseration may expel,   10
But mercy, Faustus, of thy saviour sweet,
Whose blood alone must wash away thy guilt.

Printed in Great Britain by Cox & Wyman Limited
London · Reading · Fakenham